"KITTY STRYKER HAS FOLLOWED UP HER POWERFUL BOOK on consent culture with an essential resource for young people. *Say More* is crystal clear and complex without being dense or academic and is brimming with compassion and identification… It will change the game for many young people and parents, whether dealing with extreme situations or the everyday challenges of interpersonal relationships and maintaining one's agency."

—ALEX WINTER, ACTOR,
Bill & Ted's Excellent Adventure

"KITTY STRYKER IS THE PERFECT COMPANION WITH WHOM to properly tuck into the important, intelligent, meaty conversations young people want and need to have about consent…Nothing's rushed over, and nothing's hushed up. *Say More* truly gets into the nitty gritty, so readers emerge not only with a more profound understanding of what navigating consent can look like, but also with a toolkit of skills to help them do so with greater confidence, comfort and safety."

—ALIX FOX, SEXUAL CULTURE WRITER AND SCRIPT
consultant to Netflix's *Sex Education*

"*SAY MORE* IS AN EARNEST, FUNNY, THOUGHT-PROVOKING exploration into not just consent, but good communication as a whole. The book approaches navigating consent with a blend of sensitivity and unapologetic, straightforward clarity, making it an essential read for anyone—not just teens—looking to enhance their communication skills. Kitty's emphasis on authenticity and compassion makes it a standout addition to the conversation. This book belongs in every sex-ed classroom and every relationship therapist's office."

—CATE OSBORN (CATIEOSAURUS),
certified ADHD sex educator

"SAY MORE IS A BRILLIANT OVERVIEW OF ALL THINGS consent. It gives teens spot-on, realistic advice about how we might navigate all our relationships more consensually, and about how to handle things when we, inevitably, don't manage it at times. Kitty Stryker is just the friendly mentor required to guide us through this complex territory with clarity, steadiness, and a whole lot of relatable experience."

—DR. MEG-JOHN BARKER, CO-AUTHOR OF
How To Understand Your Sexuality and
Sexuality: A Graphic Guide

"KITTY STRYKER DIVES INTO THE COMPLEXITIES AND nuances of consent while giving straightforward and concise information and advice on how to navigate it all. I think teens will find this book more like a talk with a big sister than a 'how to' book on consent. Each chapter tackles tough questions that we all wrestle with. I wish I could have read a book like this when I was a teen!

—ERICA SCOTT, CO-AUTHOR OF
*Creating Consent Culture:
A Handbook for Educators* and founder of
Creating Consent Culture

SAY MORE

CONSENT CONVERSATIONS FOR TEENS

KITTY STRYKER

THORNAPPLE
PRESS

Say More:

Consent Conversations for Teens

Thornapple Press
300 – 722 Cormorant Street
Victoria, BC V8W 1P8 Canada
press@thornapplepress.ca

Thornapple Press is a brand of Talk Science to Me Communications Inc. and the successor to Thorntree Press. Our business offices are located in the traditional, ancestral and unceded territories of the ləkʷəŋən and W̱SÁNEĆ peoples.

Cover and interior design by Jeff Werner
Substantive editing by Andrea Zanin
Copy-editing by Heather van der Hoop
Proofreading by Alison Whyte

Library and Archives Canada Cataloguing in Publication

Title: Say more : consent conversations for teens / Kitty Stryker.
Names: Stryker, Kitty, 1984- author.
Description: Includes bibliographical references.
Identifiers: Canadiana (print) 20230584756 |
Canadiana (ebook) 20230584764 | ISBN 9781990869518 (softcover) |
ISBN 9781990869525 (EPUB)
Subjects: LCSH: Sexual consent. | LCSH: Sex instruction for teenagers.
Classification: LCC HQ35 .S77 2024 | DDC 613.9071/2–dc23

10 9 8 7 6 5 4 3 2 1

Printed in the United States of America.

THIS BOOK IS DEDICATED TO MY PARENTS,
who taught me autonomy and
accountability (even when it was hard).

Thank you for always having my back.
I love you <3

CONTENTS

CONSENTING SHOULD BE PRETTY EASY, RIGHT?

Asking for things we want, telling people things we need or don't want, or saying yes or no to things someone else wants: it isn't really *that* complicated, is it? If someone else gave you this book, it may even seem so simple, you may be wondering why they think you need to read this in the first place.

Look, in some situations, it blessedly really *is* that simple, and few of us probably do need a book about it. Let's say I'm getting a sandwich and the guy behind the counter asks if I want onions. I don't, so I say no thanks, and he just moves on and asks me about tomatoes. No big deal. Or maybe someone offers you a cup of tea, and you just need to say if you want it or not, and if you do, if you want lemon with it or not. Easy peasy.

But so many of our interactions with each other, even just the way we think about (or don't think about!) our interactions with each other, are a whole lot more complicated than what someone wants on their sandwich, or whether somebody wants tea. Heck, even *those* kinds of interactions can be trickier sometimes than they may seem.

What about when the offer of tea is from your grandma, who is just awful to be around, even for the amount of time it takes to drink a cup of tea? What if, on top of that, what you say to your grandma, and whether you spend time with her or not, impacts your relationship with one of your parents? What about if your college tuition getting paid has to do with having tea or not?

What about when the person making that sandwich, for who knows what reason, apparently wants to put onions on it so flipping bad he will not stop pushing the onions, will not take what should be an easy "no thanks" to something as seemingly simple as onions? You might find yourself just saying yes to the onions you do not want just to get the darn sandwich already and get the heck outta there, away from the sandwich guy. (And yes, if this scenarios sounds familiar, it absolutely can and often does happen when it's about our bodies or sex, not onions.)

Even what might appear on the surface as an easy situation with asking, boundaries or communication between people can be anywhere from a little more complicated than it seems to very, very loaded and complex, depending on the whole context of what's going on, right down to it merely happening in this very complex world we all live in. This is all often a lot more complicated and confusing than many people want to even think about, let alone talk about. Not Kitty Stryker, though.

I remember the first time I heard of her, over 15 years ago, when she was a younger person working very hard to create conversations about consent within the BDSM communities in San Francisco, and facing quite a lot of backlash. My first impression of her was that she was very brave, very honest and very generous. Brave because it takes a lot of guts to talk to people about consent in a group where quite a lot of them insist they already have it all down and that anyone who doesn't think so is the problem. Honest because she was telling the truth, even to folks who really didn't want to hear it. Generous because being willing to open yourself up to the kind of backlash that Kitty faced and keep on for the sake of everyone's safety and well-being is an incredible service to your community and beyond.

These qualities, and Kitty's experience with talking about consent and everything that goes with it, are just a few reasons why I think you're so lucky to have her as a guide in learning about all of this. Kitty absolutely understands that while sometimes it's as easy as just saying no to tea or onions, more often than not, it's not so easy at all—and many times, especially in often-loaded situations like sexual encounters or relationships with power disparities, it can be really challenging and overwhelming.

She knows that it's not easy at all in cultures, great or small, where a lack of consent, or even outright nonconsent, is the rule, not the exception. It's not easy when so many of us weren't raised in cultures of consent, and when *not* being asked or even really considered—if we want to be hugged or kissed, if we want to go somewhere, if it's OK if someone cleans our space without us there, if it's OK for someone to look under our clothes at a part of our body—was what was normal for us. It's for sure not easy if and when we don't even know words or terms for some of the most basic ways we've already had interactions where consent has and hasn't been present in the first place.

It's not as easy to understand consent when so much of what we've seen in popular representations of places where consent needs to be happening—like touching each other, sex, even just doing chores—shows us zero of the consent part, and may even falsely or lazily, and for sure irresponsibly, represent *non*consent as consent. It's not easy in situations where we want someone to like us, or we think that asking for consent will zap all the magic from the moment. It's not easy if we've said yes to something before, if someone seems annoyed with us or if we aren't even 100% sure of what we actually do and don't want in the first place. It's incredibly difficult if a relationship we're already deep in has its own culture of nonconsent, or if we grew up being told that when someone loved us, they were supposed to just do anything we wanted or vice versa, and doing otherwise means they don't love us or we must not love them.

It's not as easy when the people involved are people we have much more complex feelings about and relationships with than the dude making the sandwich: a new, but very desperately wanted friend; our parents or grandparents; a teacher; a crush; a boyfriend, girlfriend or other kind of paramour. It's not easy if and when, as it so often does in this world, some part of consent or the process of it feels like a moratorium on some really important part of who we are: our gender, our orientation, our maturity, our strength, our lovability, our attractiveness or even our worth and value as a whole person, full stop. It's really, really freaking hard when we're scared, as we can so often feel, to ask someone else for something we want, or to answer someone who's asking, when we don't even feel basically safe in an ask, an answer, a calling in or out, or even just in having a consent conversation.

Kitty Stryker really, really gets all this, and she's got you.

She's been deeply dedicated to helping people learn to do better with consent and building consent culture for a long time now, and from what I can tell, she's never stopped caring really deeply about that work, not even for a minute. She gets that it's complicated and that there often aren't easy answers or ways to do things. She gets how much bigger this is than just yes or no, want or don't want, should have or shouldn't have: there are layers, and side roads, and super-nuanced interplay and whole bigger systems we have to often navigate in the process—systems we might not even be able to wrap our heads around and that we are maybe at the very beginning of understanding—of what might otherwise seem like pretty simple interactions. In this book, she doesn't just offer help for the person being asked, like so much mainstream consent information does, and she makes sure to include information for people who have violated boundaries—an uncommon and important honesty in recognizing that at one time or another, in one way or another, that will be all of us, and probably way more than once. She also writes this book knowing that young people, in particular, don't just need help with navigating consent and boundaries with possible sex partners or friends, but also usually need help and support when it comes to handling situations with people in their lives who have agency they just don't: parents and other adults with authority. In all of these areas, Kitty talks you through the considerations with candor and care, and offers practical and super-helpful tools so that you can bring, improve and build consent culture into your life and world in a real way, and actually learn *how* to do so, not just that you should want to.

Boundaries, limits, consent, communication in relationships: none of these are usually anywhere near as easy as they can seem on the surface. But they are navigable, and it is often easier to get better at them—or even learn to be really good at them!—than it may seem. What you've got in your hands right here is a top-notch set of tools; some real, vulnerable and deep thinking; and a truly great and dedicated guide bringing everything she knows from over a decade of hard work with the sole intention of helping you, just where you are in life, navigate it and build a very real consent culture for yourself, for your life, for everyone around you and, in your own way, for the whole rest of the world (sandwich guy and grandma very much included).

Heather Corinna
FOUNDER OF SCARLETEEN

NOTE TO ADULTS

HI THERE, ADULT HUMAN! THANKS FOR CHECKING OUT this introduction to consent culture for teens—it's really great that you want a youth in your life to learn these tools to help them navigate this topic. I don't know about you, but I'm still learning a lot about what "consent" means in theory and in application. It's a deceptively complex topic, even for adults!

Say More is intended to be part mentorship, part critical-thinking guide, part self-exploration, part challenge to the things we learn culturally as "just how it is." Hopefully, it's written in a way that's accessible, and I use personal experiences to illustrate that it's OK to find consent complicated and hard, because it *is* complicated and hard!

I want to acknowledge that I am not a caregiver to a teen. I can't speak to the joys and tribulations that impact the lives of those who are. But I *have* been a teenager before, and I can speak to what I remember from that time.

While I know it may be tempting to check up on the teen you give this book to, in order to see if they're looking through it, read their responses to the questions, etc., I would gently ask that you let them explore this book at their own pace, in their own time. These are intense topics, and it can be overwhelming and scary to explore these questions. They might whip through the book in a couple of weeks, or it might take them months. Both are OK! Let them figure out how to use this material and come to you with their questions and thoughts. I think they're more aware of consent and related topics than many of us were as teens. It's so amazing to see.

People learn by osmosis more than we realize, I think. When the teen in your life sees you give them this book in good faith, believe in them and trust in their process, they replicate that in their own relationships. It's really important for us to model the consent culture we want to see in the world!

That said, many youth are waiting to hear from their parents when it comes to conversations about consent, including and especially when it comes to sex and relationships. Out of respect (and maybe a lot of anxiety), many parents are waiting for their teens to approach them. Someone has to go first, but how can you do that in a way that also recognizes and honors the awkwardness? Personally, I like to ask if I can bring up something a little uncomfortable, and offer them the ability to opt out if and when they choose. Then, rather than asking a question about what the other person is doing or what they understand, I talk about something I found complicated or weird when I was growing up. This vulnerability enables the listener to meet me in that raw and curious space—and it might work for you, too.

Once teens feel comfortable asking questions, they bring up really interesting and complex dilemmas! The questions I chose to write about in this book all came from teenagers. And if I'm honest, I've heard these same questions from adults my age. They're very human questions, spoken with vulnerability and a desire to do better. If you trust the teens in your life to want to do this kind of introspection, I think they'll come through and surprise you.

Thank you for trusting them—and thank you for trusting me to offer this experience to the next generations.

—Kitty Stryker

ACKNOWLEDGMENTS

I HAVE TO THANK SO MANY PEOPLE FOR OFFERING ADVICE as I worked on this book! This was a project that had a fast turnaround time and I was able to achieve it in part because I had so much excellent support from my community.

Thank you especially to the teens who responded to my survey and guided me on which questions to specifically address in this book—you were vulnerable and honest, and I hope I provided you with the skills you need to navigate the world and consent!

Thank you to Avens O'Brien for being my ethical checkpoint as I tackle these issues (and life, generally). I appreciate and love you!

Thank you to my dad, who is always available for phone calls and emotional support while I'm writing. And thanks to my mum, who battled fatphobia in healthcare and lost—may she rest in power.

Thank you to Erika, Dylan, S., Sid, Synnora, Shiloh, Jeremy, Melanie and other caregivers who read through drafts, offered follow-up questions and helped me fine-tune the language.

Thank you to my sponsor Nazelah, my house-mate Quin, my life partner Cinnamon and my friend

Miriam for making sure I took care of myself during this process!

Thank you to Thornapple Press for taking a chance on me and giving me another book to write right off the bat! It was a fun challenge, and sorely needed by the community.

And of course, special thanks to the best co-writers, Camus and Bataille, my sweet cats who kept me on task by sleeping on my laptop and biting my toes.

INTRODUCTION

FIRST OF ALL, HI! I'M KITTY, AND THANKS FOR PICKING up my book on consent. I'm an author, an activist and the founder of the website ConsentCulture. com. I've been doing the work of trying to understand what consent really is, how to communicate it and why it's such a sticky subject for over 13 years, and I'm still learning more about it (and myself) every day.

In my edited anthology, *Ask: Building Consent Culture*, I asked people from all walks of life to write about consent culture from a variety of perspectives: why "consenting to harm" can be a struggle for professional wrestlers, or what consent looks like when you're Black and pregnant in a hospital staffed by white folks, or whose consent matters when you're a teen and rely on parents to sign off on your gender-affirming medical care. And in *Ask Yourself: The Consent Culture Workbook*, I wanted to raise questions about what consent really means with other adults, encouraging them to poke at the frayed edges of what autonomy means in a society that is restricted by many bigotries and judgments.

This book is my attempt to take those ideas and blend them into a smoothie for teen consumption, not as a way of talking down to you, but as a way to make these scenarios more relatable to your lives.

It's awesome that you're choosing to learn about this topic, especially when it's such a tangled mess of a thing to tackle. It feels like everyone has a really strong opinion on it, until it comes to actually addressing some of the tough questions…and that's not especially helpful when you're the one with the tough questions. We hear that consent is important for healthier relationships, but not a lot on how to actually practice it, or why it matters, other than "because I said so." Having once been a teenager myself, I know how annoyingly dismissive that feels.

I'm here to try and help guide you through some of that, not by telling you what to think or what to do, but by helping you figure out what makes the most sense *to you*. The questions in this book all came from teens like you, muddling through social interactions trying to be A Good Person, not entirely sure what makes a person "good." It's hard stuff, and frankly, I think a lot of adults avoid getting into it because they don't really know the answers themselves! So it's great that you're here exploring it.

Let's address the elephant in the room: consent is tough.

We're told it's incredibly important, while also being given mixed messages about when it's valid and when it isn't and very little education about how to interact with it. Sex education often offers some simple bumper-sticker phrases like "yes means yes," but doesn't get explicit about what that looks like in practice. Power dynamics are often ignored entirely, and when they are discussed, it's usually as a warning rather than as a way to think critically and troubleshoot. Never mind thinking about consent as it pertains to things outside of dating relationships! How might consent impact your friendships? Where does enthusiastic consent fit in when it comes to doing homework or chores? What about consent when it comes to doing what you want vs. pleasing the adults in your life? These aren't typically areas we discuss relative to consent, yet I think they're all interlinked.

I also think being a teenager grappling with consent is in many ways especially complicated. On the one hand, you're experiencing more advanced situations for the first time—sex, substance use, how to balance school and a social life, reward now vs. reward later. You're almost an adult, almost on your own, but you also aren't, yet; you probably live with a caretaker you're expected to listen to and follow directions from. I remember this clash from when I was a teen being raised by anarchist parents (and don't worry, you'll get to read about that!).

No regrets, right, Dad?

So what exactly is "consent culture"? For me, it's the idea of a culture where consent is a core ethic, a guiding principle. I think about consent culture as in opposition to not just boundary crossing or entitlement, but fear. When I talk about consent culture, the thing I see come up for people when they react is fear. They're afraid of doing something wrong, afraid they've already done something wrong, afraid they'll be cast out from their community without even knowing they messed up. Sometimes, they're afraid of what their lives would be like without the unspoken advantages they benefit from: being white, male, cisgender, straight. They're afraid that naming these privileges will cause them to lose something that makes them feel comfortable. They're afraid that consent culture is a club with which I plan to bludgeon them.

I think of consent culture in many ways as the opposite of fear. To have a culture centered on consent relies on trust. You have to trust that people, for the most part, are not trying to harm each other. Sometimes you might get hurt, and it won't be on purpose, but it'll hurt just the same. Consent culture at my purest ideal embraces that good faith and allows for accountability to be a place for growth. For something like consent culture to work, you have to be surrounded by people you can build trust with, even when it's scary and hard.

And when you have that kind of support, it makes it much easier to recognize and weed out people who don't have good intentions.

This book is not intended to be a lecture, or a list of rules to follow so you don't ever mess up. It's more about knowing what kinds of questions to ask yourself and those around you, so you can make better, more informed decisions. My hope is that this book can be a resource to help you think critically about how you were raised, the peer pressures you experience, your own conflicting feelings between heart and head (and, more often than not, hormones!). It is intended to shed light on some situations that we don't often get to talk about in depth, so you can navigate your own consent, as well as better interpret other people's.

Now, I'm not a teen, but I wanted to make sure that I wasn't approaching this topic as some kind of finger-wagging lecture. Therefore, when I was putting this book together, I asked caregivers and the teens in their lives to fill out an informal survey about what they knew about consent, what questions they had, and what sorts of activities would be most useful for them. The questions I use as prompts throughout are all questions teens like you asked within that survey, questions they were hoping to answer. Many of them are also questions I get from adults twice your age! They're good questions with complicated and individual answers. As such, I don't think there's One Right Way to answer them. Some might bring up your lived experiences, while others may bring up ideals: how you'd like to handle such a situation if you came across it. When answering, trust your instincts. You are the number-one expert on you—and it's absolutely OK for your experiences to be different from mine. Your autonomy is ultimately your own.

You may choose to go through this book in order and answer one prompt at a time. You might skip around to the questions you've been wrestling with the most. You might read a few of the stories before deciding where you want to dip in further. All of those options are valid ways to explore this material; *Say More* is meant to be a tool for you to pick up and use as needed.

Answering a question may bring up a lot of feelings, so let me reassure you: there's no right way to go through this book, and no deadlines for when you have to complete it. One of the first lessons about knowing yourself and your own consent is that you can do this work however you want, for however long you want. You might want to talk about these questions with your friends, or with family, or with a therapist, or even just journal about it and keep it to yourself. It's all good. Part of the reason I wanted to call this book "consent conversations for teens" is because I didn't want it to be a series of essay prompts that feel like homework—it's a conversation between author and reader, between you and your loved ones, and ultimately, with yourself.

This book isn't a university class, so I tried to steer away from studies and citations. I also don't want you to take anything I say in here as the One True Answer; rather, my goal is to present you with some things to think about, so that you can come to your own informed conclusions. The relevant studies I was able to dig up around topics of consent and communication and coercion included overwhelmingly heterosexual, white, cisgender participants. They also focused on either exclusively "sexual consent" or consent within the medical field, where body language and informed consent take on a whole different context. The available information is imperfect, incomplete and inherently somewhat skewed, so I didn't want to use academic studies as the basis for these discussions. That said, I do recommend that you look up some of these studies if you'd like to learn more, but always with a critical eye for the context in which they were done, who paid for them and the sample sizes.

It may feel intimidating that there isn't one right answer to these questions. It's scary to sit with the idea that we have probably crossed a boundary sometime in our lives, and we likely will again. But how exciting to be humble in that knowledge, to accept our fallibility and, instead of succumbing to despair and apathy, want to strive to get as close to 100% consent as is possible! How thrilling to seek to hurt each other (and ourselves) less! And to be honest, how amazingly cool that you're doing this work as a teenager. Good for you! A lot of adults struggle to do this stuff, so give yourself a pat on the back for picking up this book.

All of this anxiety and uncertainty is why I wanted to encourage us, adults and teens together, to "say more." OK, I'll admit part of it is me trying to be clever about the slang "say less" as a way of showing agreement, and I apologize for having my "how do you do, fellow kids" moment. But I really do think we should "say more" to ask more questions, to explain our thought processes, to really try to understand why we think what we think and why others think the way they think. There are a lot of things we just assume about ourselves and each other that maybe deserve a second look, and I'm hoping this book encourages you to do just that.

Consent culture, in my mind, is less like a rigid foundation, staying in one place and crumbling when pushed. It's more like a bridge, flexible yet secure, bringing people from our current lifetime toward a better future.

Won't you join me on the other side?

WHY DOES CONSENT FEEL SO WEIRD?

SOMETHING I HEAR OFTEN, FROM ADULTS AND TEENS alike, is, "consent is so clearly important—so why does it feel so *weird*?"

I think one of the reasons consent feels kind of awkward and weird is that we don't have a really solid, unchanging definition for it. Every person I've ever spoken to about consent has felt pretty sure they knew what the word meant, but when I asked for a definition, they found it hard to pin down. We've heard really simple ideas about consent—"yes means yes," for example, and "no means no"—but what about when your parents tell you to do your homework or you can't go to the movies with your friends? Are you consenting to do your homework? Is it a type of coercion? It may not be *force*, but even so, it's also not entirely uninfluenced consent. And sometimes, there is an abusive dynamic that goes beyond the usual struggles as teens develop their independence; some parents and other adults do use force and violence and threats to get people to do what they want (and if you're not sure if you're in an abusive situation, Scarleteen is a great place to look into that more—check the Resources section at the end of the book). Where do situations like these fit into the definition of consent?

This is going to sound out of left field, but bear with me for a second.

I used to feel really sure that I knew what a fish was. Swims in the water. Has gills. Spawns eggs. Has bones. A fish, right?

Then I started listening to a podcast called *Let's Learn Everything!* and I discovered that what is commonly called a fish actually spans several types of aquatic animals, from sharks to manta rays to lampreys to coelacanths. While many fish live in the water, some, like the walking catfish, can spend a significant amount of time out of the water. While many fish have gills and use them to breathe, others, like lungfish, use lungs instead. Fish are often cold-blooded—except for tuna, which are actually warm-blooded. Scientists have a really difficult time making a definition of "fish" that doesn't end up including some non-fish, or leaving out some animals we would call "fish."

Then there's the issue of cultural definitions. For example, the Catholic Church used to consider beavers to be fish for the purposes of Lent (they believe in not eating warm-blooded animals during that religious period). The popular, always chilled-out capybara was also a semi-skilled swimmer, and so became classified as a "fish" for the purposes of religious mealtimes. Capybara is still a popular meal to have during Lent in Venezuela, despite the fact that most people would not consider the largest rodent in the world a fish!

I think "fish" is a really good example of how we as humans sometimes believe that our definition of a concept is universal when it's actually imperfect and incomplete, and maybe always will be. I like to say I think of consent as a living document; my understanding of and relationship to consent is constantly being refined and expanded as I learn new things about myself and how I interact with the world.

We all know that rape culture is bad, so therefore consent culture must be good, right? Yes means yes and no means no, after all. Why is all of this so complicated? Why isn't there a formulaic solution for these conundrums of how to ascertain consent?

There are a lot of reasons for why the conversation around even defining consent, what it impacts and what it doesn't cover, is ongoing and complex. For a start, cultural norms help to shape communication styles. For example, in some cultures, eating everything on your plate is a nonverbal signal that you are still hungry, while in other cultures, if you *don't* eat everything on your plate, it means you didn't like the meal. No wonder people get their wires crossed!

Another factor that can add complexity to this conversation is individualism vs. collectivism. In the United States, the idea of personal freedom is considered a core value by many people. In Japan, meanwhile, collectivism and knowing your role as part of a harmonious group is a core value. Both beliefs have some validity, and both have their shortcomings, especially when it comes to consent. While an American person may feel that protecting their personal ability to choose is more important than following the will of a group, a Japanese person may feel their fulfillment of their role as part of a community is more important than individual choice. These two people will likely define consent differently, as they each have a different lens through which they see the world.

Yet when we talk about consent, we often neglect to make sure that we're all talking about the same thing. It's difficult to be aware of your bias until you make a concerted effort to unpack it, but that's a vital aspect of this kind of work. Culture, upbringing, religion, ethnicity, politics, gender, physical and mental health—all of these factors add layers of understanding to a concept as amorphous as "consent."

And if we don't all have the same definition of consent, how could we possibly look for one easy answer that would work in all circumstances?

Humans often want to have certainty. There is a sense of security when we have static, universal understandings. Unfortunately, that certainty comes at a hefty price, one where we are constantly hearing mixed messages about what is and isn't OK. When it comes to the idea of "consent," we are constantly bumping up against inconsistencies about what consent is, when it matters and how to communicate about it. I think that's one of the reasons consent can feel kind of weird.

We're going to talk about the complexity of consent, and I'm not here to give you definite answers. Our relationship to consent is a conversation we have with ourselves, and a conversation we have with the people in our lives. It's fully individual, even if there's often overlap. My goal here is to help you stretch your muscles a little, so that it doesn't feel intensely weird forever.

> **Think of a time you felt a way you would define now as "weird" (whether that be awkward, or uncomfortable, or ashamed). What does that feel like to you?**

How do you feel "weird" in your body? What goes through your brain when you feel it?

Have you ever felt "weird" doing something the first few times, but then it didn't feel that way anymore? What was that like?

Also, while we're talking about definitions, what does consent mean to you? What are some scenarios you can think of related to consent that aren't about dating? Does thinking of them change your initial definition of consent?

WHY IS CONSENT SO COMPLICATED?

ANOTHER REASON I THINK CONSENT CAN FEEL WEIRD? We're not really used to having frank conversations about...well, anything, really, especially when it comes to feelings, even more so if they have anything to do with sexuality. Whether schools can teach teens about safer sex or the existence of LGBTQ+ people varies from place to place, never mind whether they're allowed to facilitate even more awkward conversations about masturbation or pleasure. Social media platforms often won't let educators talk about consent, because they deem it too obscene! With something so vital and important treated like a taboo, no wonder talking about it honestly feels uncomfortable.

The fact that we don't talk explicitly about these topics doesn't mean we aren't picking stuff up, though. There are so many ways in which unspoken expectations become rooted in us through repeated exposure in the media and reflection in our day-to-day lives. Even when we do talk about the lessons we learn about relationships from popular culture, we usually mean Disney movies and Top 40 music, which don't always align with consent best practices.

Let me give you an example. One story that really impacted me was the idea that for consent to be valid, it needed to be enthusiastic—not just a "yes" but a "fuck yes." Early on in my consent activism, I really appreciated the idea of "yes means yes" going around colleges, focusing on getting and giving a clear affirmative instead of waiting to hear a "no."

That said, I also began to realize that consent could still be valid even if it was unenthusiastic. While it was useful for me to reflect on whether my yes was a "fuck yes" or an "eh, OK," the story that consent was only "real" if it was wholeheartedly positive was not one that served me. After all, I worked retail at the mall, and I certainly wasn't saying "fuck yes" every time I had to clock in! Moreover, no one expected that my consent at work was enthusiastic. No one really cared about whether I consented to work at all, but my landlord certainly cared about me paying my bills! Or when my dentist asked me to come in at 8 a.m. to finish my root canal, I agreed, even though I hate being up early and also hate going to the dentist. The end result was something I wanted, therefore I said yes, but I can promise you I wasn't *enthusiastic* about it!

Exploring these scenarios gave me a much more nuanced and complicated understanding of consent, and made me think a lot about *why* that story ("yes means yes") was so important to me. I wanted the security of clarity, the safety of not feeling differently about a situation later. But even an enthusiastic yes in the moment can feel different down the line with more context, and accepting that was important for me in understanding some of my own difficult experiences.

It's hard to know what to think or how to feel when the ground keeps shifting underneath you. "Consent is key!" my parents would tell me, before insisting I had to do my homework before I could hang out with my friends. "Your body is your own!" the day care center would tell us, and then they'd tell us we had to hug it out if we had an argument with another kid on the playground. It seemed like I would get told one thing, that I had autonomy over my body and could say no, but then I'd be told that I wasn't old enough to make those choices. I was told that I didn't *really* understand the impact of certain choices, but then these adults never really explained that impact to me, either.

Here's something adults really struggle with admitting: at age 18, you are not magically imbued with knowledge and self-confidence that enable you to make fully consensual decisions about sex, the military, tattoos and voting, uninfluenced by the world around you. It just doesn't happen like that. I have met incredibly self-aware teenagers, and wildly insecure 40-year-olds. Hell, I'm still figuring stuff out and I teach people about consent! The laws we have in place exist because there is a need for some sort of limit to be legally spelled out, hopefully to protect the majority of vulnerable people from being taken advantage of. But people take advantage of each other perfectly legally all the time, and also laws aren't perfect, either in how they're written or in how they're enforced.

Please scream inside your heart.

That's part of why this is all so complicated. Talking about consent has tendrils connected to so many other social expectations: about when a child becomes an adult, about mindfulness and awareness when under the influence of alcohol or other substances, about your responsibilities vs. your desires, about what constitutes respect for other people. To talk honestly about consent is to own up to all of the other stories you've taken in, which inform your ethics, your culture and how you see yourself in relationship to the world. And that's a complicated, constantly shifting thing!

Does the fact that it's complicated, and perhaps on some level unknowable, mean it's not worth interrogating and exploring? I don't think so. In the scientific method, one of the things that you're always trying to do is disprove your own hypothesis in order to feel more certain of what is truth. In that same spirit, it's actually really fun to challenge my own beliefs, adding new information that deepens my understanding of why this and not that. Hopefully you also have a curious mind, and that's why you're here! But also? It's OK to feel a little overwhelmed. I think we all feel that way sometimes, even if we're shy about admitting it.

We all live in a culture of stories that influence how we interpret the world, like the value of the American Dream, how to tell if someone really likes you or what makes a person beautiful. What are some of the stories you've heard from your family, the media you consume for entertainment or the news that impact your understanding of consent?

How do these stories serve you?

How do they hold you back?

Have those stories changed as you've gotten older?

Do you interpret the stories differently in some way now (like, did you find Sleeping Beauty romantic as a little kid, but now you're a little grossed out)?

WHY IS CONSENT SO OFTEN TREATED AS A GENDERED THING?

CONTENT WARNING: THIS CHAPTER TOUCHES ON SEXUAL assault.

You've probably encountered one of these tropes before in a TV show or a movie: "shut up and kiss me," "wearing someone down until they date you," "surprise kiss they're mad about and then melt into," "he said, she said." There are so many examples of questionable or full-on romanticized nonconsent in media that it would take hours to list them all. While long-time perpetrator Disney is starting to reconsider its part in this cultural programming—in the recent live-action *The Little Mermaid*, the song "Kiss the Girl" now includes lyrics telling Prince Eric to ask Ariel before kissing her—there are still plenty of examples of crossing boundaries being presented as romantic or proof of chemistry.

Consent has often socially been treated as something women give and men take, through either force or cajoling. I have a small vintage book from 1951 called *Girls Men Choose* by Richard D. Strieby, and its yellowed pages offer this gem:

> *If you "know all the answers," keep them well concealed. Let him take the initiative, and keep it. If he does not seem inclined to take the initiative, force it upon him, by being incapable of taking it. For some men, this may be difficult at first, but if you constantly depend upon his decisions and judgment, he will respond by assuming the positive, masculine role, and liking it.*

While it may not surprise you to see advice like this given to teenagers in the 1950s, I've seen similar advice (albeit worded slightly differently) given even now on Instagram and TikTok. "Let him take the lead," some relationship advice columns say, "and you'll get him hooked!" This is not only bad advice (not all men want to take the lead, for a start), but it lays the groundwork for a really toxic dynamic in which men are trying to "win" through acting, not asking, and women are trying to "entice" by playing subtle mind games. Also, not only does this advice expect that everyone is heterosexual, it creates a cat-and-mouse kind of situation where you're competing with each other, not cooperating. And that's not only exhausting, it's kind of gross!

Unfortunately, something being kind of gross rarely stops it from being a commonly accepted "truth." In many ways, consent is still discussed and even taught as a terrible, heterosexual game of chess. It's treated as inevitable that women are gate-keepers who get punished for having sex "wrong" (too soon and you're a slut, not soon enough and you're a prude), while men are initiators, rewarded and praised for being sexual and "going for it" rather than checking in. These expectations can then impact how we understand a story about a situation of unclear consent, or even how we create our own stories. And then we end up with ad campaigns trying to raise awareness about sexual violence (a good and worthy goal!) that portray people crossing boundaries as male or masculine, and those having their boundaries crossed as female or feminine. This framing reinforces those gendered cultural norms without any recognition that boundary crossing (or having your boundaries crossed!) is not a gendered experience. Or even strictly a sexual or romantic experience.

Now, this issue persists in part because of years and years of social expectations that treated women as the property of men and ignored, fetishized or demonized the existence of queer, nonbinary and trans people. Legal and social misogyny (the hatred of women) absolutely impacted women's ability to consent, and still does. For example, "what was she wearing?" is still a phrase that comes up in courtrooms as a way to hand-wave away legal consequences for sexual assault, as if what you wear makes you more or less deserving of bodily autonomy. Going into misogyny and consent in more detail is a whole other book, but check out the Resources section if you want to learn more about these topics.

One thing I want to point out here is that these narrow definitions have also negatively impacted men, and continue to. For years, the legal definition of rape in the United States only acknowledged it happening to women, and then only through forced penetration. Because of that legal definition, only women were recognized as having been raped, which meant research on the topic also used that narrow definition. The biased idea that consent is something women give and men take ended up skewing many scientific studies to further underline that specific dynamic while ignoring the many other possibilities. Those studies were the basis for more studies that perpetuated the problem, while resources and awareness campaigns continued to name one particular type of sexual violence as if it was the only kind, which then silenced people whose identities and experiences didn't fit that narrative, and thus they didn't speak up in studies.

However, when the definition expanded to include a man being coerced into penetrating someone without his consent, or being penetrated without his consent, including while high or drunk, surveys began to turn up many more examples of men experiencing sexual assault. As queer, non-binary and trans people began to be recognized and identified in the data, the statistics changed yet again—but the studies are still catching up.

When researching for this book, I found many scientific studies that focused exclusively on consent within a heterosexual dynamic—which is frustrating when looking at wider demographics! I don't think it's true or helpful that a) there are only two genders or b) one is the aggressive gender and one is the passive gender. Sure, sexism can be one reason why someone with more social advantages feels entitled to someone else's body or time, but this sense of entitlement can also be impacted by racism, classism or any other power disparity. Consent violations are not inherently things that men do to women, or that only exist within a sexual dynamic.

In short, consent is often treated as a gendered thing because society is very, very slow to accept change, even when we know that it's harmful not to. This resistance to change impacts how we write laws, how we treat real-life victims of abuse, how we tell fictional stories about love and sex, and, of course, the norms we reinforce with each other in everyday social situations. What I'm hoping to do with this book is encourage critical thinking across the board—not only about what you see and hear in your day-to-day life, but also when you hear someone say "studies say…" Ask which studies, and read them. Figure out who funded the study, and what kinds of studies these scientists tend to run. What was the sample size? Who did the study include, and who wasn't included? Ask questions, and stay curious. And always be open to data that doesn't fit with what you've learned so far!

What are some gendered beliefs around consent that you've encountered?

Do you find them to be accurate in your day-to-day life?

Can you think of an example of a time when those beliefs were proven wrong?

If you hear someone stating one of these outdated gendered beliefs as if it's fact, how could you respond?

HOW DO WE NORMALIZE CONSENT IN OUR CULTURE?

ONE OF THE REASONS I STARTED USING THE PHRASE "consent culture" so frequently is that I noticed when people talked about consent and boundary crossing, it was often about *avoiding* rape culture. We're encouraged to speak out when friends make jokes about prison rape or other sexual assaults, telling them that kind of humor is pretty gross, actually. We're told not to publicly defend celebrities accused of sexual assault or other violence, especially when that involves denouncing the victims. And those are good, important things to do—and hard things to do! God knows I often felt like a killjoy by taking a firm stand against rape culture as a teenager. I was accused a lot of not having a sense of humor. I learned to respond, wide-eyed, "Oh, OK! Can you explain the joke, then? I don't get it," which often shut people up.

There are a lot of good resources out there for learning how to recognize and stand up to entitlement culture in our society, and it's certainly something we still need help with. But I wonder sometimes if in focusing so much time and energy on what people *shouldn't* be doing, we aren't really spending any time guiding them on what they *should* do instead. I think that's equally important, to give people something to strive toward, not just something to steer clear of.

Now, let's be real. We are individuals, and thus our impact on the wide world of "culture" is reasonably limited. I'm not going to give you suggestions on how you can change the world, because frankly that's a lot of pressure and not entirely realistic. But what I will do is give you some ideas of things you can do in *your* world, in your community, with your friends, that might have a ripple effect.

One major shift that sounds so simple but ended up being surprisingly complicated for me is around hugging. I know, I'm sure you've heard the discussions about not making kids hug the grandparents if they don't want to. Even so, and even in a community of people who said they cared about consent and would never make their kids hug a family member they didn't want to, I found myself getting hugged, awkwardly, rather a lot when I moved to California. I'd meet someone new and introduce myself with an extended hand (a nonverbal cue that I wanted to shake hands!) and people would brush my hand aside, saying

"Oh, *I'm a hugger*" and swoop in before I could say anything. I absolutely hated it but assumed that I had to just put up with it because that's what Californians do.

Then I started to assert myself. When someone said "Oh, I'm a hugger," I would put my hand out, palm in a "stop" position, and say a little more loudly, "That's great! I'm not; let's shake hands." My hand became a nonverbal but physical barrier between my body and the other person's, and my verbal disinterest in a hug was very distinct and clear. People were startled at first, but as I kept doing it, people who knew me began to approach me, arms outstretched but near their sides, asking "Would you like a hug?" Soon everyone was doing it, and the cultural norm of hugging without asking had changed. Now, as we begin to figure out cultural norms in the wake of COVID, I think that kind of assumed physical touch is less assumed anyway, so maybe this is less of an issue for you. I think it still illustrates how standing up for yourself in a kind but firm way can ripple out and impact a community, without that even being your intention.

Now, that's a very clear and physical example, but what about if a friend of yours posts something on their friends-only social media account, and you want to show another friend who doesn't have access? Normalizing consent means asking your friend before you screenshot and send their post to someone else, and to respect any limitations they give you. Or let's say you want to gush about your crush with your BFF; normalizing consent would mean asking them "Hey, can I talk about this crush for a bit?" and respecting their time, and I'd even go so far as to make sure you leave time to ask them about themselves, just so you're being fair. If the person you're dating says they don't want to watch a scary movie, normalizing consent means saying "OK!" and suggesting something else. I'm not a big fan of jump-scare movies and one of my best friends loves them. Rather than try to persuade me to change my mind, she gives me a heads-up when a movie I'm curious about has jump scares, and she watches those movies with other friends. In many ways, normalizing consent is about knowing what you want and like, and respecting what other people want and like, even if that means you don't share certain experiences.

How do we normalize consent in our culture? I think the most effective strategy I've seen has been, boringly, just to embody the consent culture I want to see in the world. I don't demand that other people do what I do, though I may choose how much time I spend with them according to how well they respect my boundaries. I speak up when I see someone pressuring another person, or when someone says something bigoted, but I've learned that yelling at people is often going to lead them to double down on their position—it just escalates things. I get listened to a lot more by just saying, "Wow, really? That's a shitty thing to say," looking disgusted and disengaging. I guess I'd say the best way I've found to normalize consent in our culture is to act like it's alien to do anything else.

Does it work? Ask me in 10 more years! I will say, though, that while it felt socially risky to stand up for myself when it came to hugging, it was really empowering to not only have my limits respected, but to see that people were overall more respectful. Often, people make shitty jokes or do shitty things because there isn't enough (or any) pushback. When you get riled up (no matter how righteously!), many people will just double down and get defensive. But when you blankly ask them to explain why the thing they did or said is good, actually, many people will realize as they explain that they were being an asshat. And you speaking up may well mean other people who don't feel confident doing so will stick by you—often, being the first to say something doesn't mean you're the only one who feels it's a bit off.

Can you think of some cultural examples (movies, music, books) where consent is ignored and the story treats that as OK and normal?

What about some examples where someone respects consent and gets teased about it?

What stories about consent might those examples teach people, and how might those stories impact their behavior?

What are some ways you could normalize consent at school? With your family? With your friends?

IS CONSENT SEXY?

ONE OF THE POPULAR PHRASES I SEE ONLINE A LOT when it comes to consent is "consent is sexy!" It always makes me sigh when I see it.

I know where that insistence comes from. For one thing, we are raised on stories about a very specific brand of "true love," where two people meet and fall in love and somehow can read each other's minds. The mind reading is how they know they are meant to be together, able to finish each other's sentences, or sandwiches, or whatever. I'm 40 years old while I write this, and I've been writing and thinking and talking about consent and culture for years (so I know better), yet even I *still* struggle with the wistful desire sometimes for a partner to just somehow *know* what I want and when I want it!

Collaborative communication isn't easy. For example, I really love flowers. My apartment is full of plants, and puttering around caring for them is one of my major joys. And yet, despite telling partners that I wish they would surprise me with flowers, they often don't, which hurts my feelings. Part of me feels like, well, I told them with my words what I want, and they still aren't doing it—can't they tell I'm frustrated at that? And yes, there is something to that feeling—a partner should listen to you, after all, about the things that matter to you. But I also have to remind myself that not everyone makes the leap from "I wish you would surprise me with flowers" to "I would like you to do this more than once, because it makes me feel heard and cared about." Spelling it out so specifically is seen as weird, and pop culture love stories tell us that we shouldn't have to do that—they'll just *know* what we want, if we're meant to be together.

This belief leads to a lot of issues elsewhere, of course. We live in a culture that often makes jokes about how asking for consent is seen as an indicator of social awkwardness, a lack of confidence, and something that definitely suggests you aren't a good couple. Saying "consent is sexy, actually!" is meant to push back against that programming.

But *is* consent sexy? And also…does it have to be?

When we protest that consent is sexy, actually, there can be an unspoken mindset that the reason consent is valid and worthy is that it is inherently related to the erotic. It centers on maintaining the steaminess of an encounter, no matter what. But what if you're sweating and anxious? What if you can't find a flirtatious way to ask if something is OK?

What about when checking in about consent just isn't sexy at all, like when someone isn't verbally responding or isn't meeting your eyes? What about when the situation isn't about sex at all, but about your friend sharing a secret you told them, or your parents entering your room when you aren't home?

Consent doesn't have to be sexy, or even about sex at all, to be important. A lot of this book is about communicating and respecting consent in different situations with different people, ranging from family members to friends to classmates working on a school project together. I think our society encourages and enables a lot of projection when it comes to nonverbal consent, suggesting it's better to ask for forgiveness than permission, and that explicitly asking leaves more space for a "no," which is seen as a bad thing. I think that's a dangerous mindset at worst, and a really sad one at best—can you imagine thinking that no one would say yes to the things you want, so you have to trick and cajole them into taking part? How depressing! And, thankfully, how untrue.

That said, I also think it's really important to recognize that one of the reasons people don't think that consent can be sexy is because they imagine a really robotic, formulaic, checkbox-marking negotiation. Most of our media pushes this idea that when the moment or behavior is right, you'll "just know." I mean, hell, a lot of media also pushes the "she starts out not liking it, but then she warms up to it" angle, which is a dangerous thing to teach people. I definitely went on dates where people recoiled when I asked if it was OK to kiss them or to hold their hand because they felt that verbalizing my desires took the magic out of them.

That's a misunderstanding waiting to happen, and it doesn't have to be so formalized and awkward! I think when people say "consent *is* sexy," what they mean is "consent *can be* sexy," and that's absolutely true!

I remember when I was a teenager on a date with this guy who was a total *Star Trek* nerd. (I continue to have a soft spot for people in glasses who can rattle off a bunch of completely fictional factoids about their favorite fan franchise.) I knew this guy was way too scared to ever even think about kissing me or holding my hand. I was definitely going to be the one making the moves! So while we were at a movie, I leaned over and whispered in his ear, "I really want to kiss you right now. What do you think about that?"

I felt his body go rigid, so I withdrew, sensing that maybe he didn't want that yet or wasn't ready (nonverbal body language!), but he whispered back, "Yes please," and we had our first kiss. It was cute, it was clear and we both leaned into it. Consent can be part of the flirtation!

I don't think you need to have a lawyer go over the rules of conduct before you interact with another person, or that you have to stop and ask, "Is this OK?" every 30 seconds. I think instead, it's helpful to be aware that excitement and discomfort can feel very similar in the body (a fluttering in the gut, a little sweatiness, flushed skin), and it's absolutely OK to go slow. It's helpful to check in when you're uncertain, and an awkward grin while you ask, "How is this for you?" can be super hot. Most importantly, people feel good when they feel comfortable, safe and respected. It takes practice, but it does get easier—and, while it may always feel a *little* squirmy, even when you're old and wrinkly, it's still better to ask for permission than forgiveness!

> **Imagine a situation where you and a crush are flirting. They're mirroring your body language, they're smiling and relaxed, and you're pretty sure you're sharing a vibe. What are some verbal and nonverbal ways you can check in and see if you're on the same page?**

What would be a clear but flirty way someone could give you the "go-ahead" for a kiss?

What are some ways you would find to be off-putting or uncomfortable?

Can you think of a situation where you had a consent conversation in a way that felt exciting and playful?

What about a time when someone asked for your consent and it felt icky? What was different about those two times (the person, the situation, the language used)?

WHEN AND HOW DO I NEED TO ASK FOR CONSENT?

I AM GENERALLY HEARTENED BY THE FACT THAT MOST people I talk to about consent really want to find some sort of guaranteed way to tell if the person they're engaging with is genuinely consenting. I think that most of the time, people really don't want to hurt each other. But when we really want a particular outcome, it's pretty human to interpret signals in a way that tells us what we want to "hear." Nonverbal communication can be a messy and confusing business, with contradictory messages and wildly varied interpretations. Verbal consent, then, feels like it would be a more reliable way to give and receive consent when we want to make sure we're on the same page. Right?

Many guides to consent tell us that we should always ask for permission before we do a new activity. When kissing, they say, you should check in again, verbally, before fondling someone's body, and again before going under the clothes, etc. While yes, ongoing enthusiastic verbal consent is the ideal, the fact is most people still prefer to use nonverbal consent or interpret inaction as consent (even when they say they believe verbal consent is the best method). And a lot of the people who are educating on interpreting body language (like pickup artists, or the "seduction community") in a romantic or sexual context are not doing so with the best of intentions; they often focus on "winning" an encounter, making romance and sex a competition rather than a collaboration. These pickup artists claim asking suggests a lack of confidence, so you should just forge ahead and deal with the consequences! Obviously, that's a miscommunication waiting to happen, with potentially dire aftereffects...so why do we as a society still believe "actions speak louder than words" when we know how easy it is to misinterpret those actions?

To make it even more complicated (I know, I'm sorry), this instinct to fall back on nonverbal communication also tends to hold true in a nonsexual context; when we watch a political debate on television or talk to a doctor about our health, we often pay attention to and trust body language over verbal communication. It's even a consideration at the workplace—as I was researching this topic, I was overwhelmed by the number of professional resources that discuss how vital vocal tone, body language and presentation of the self are when communicating to a potential employer or a client. So clearly, regardless of what we *say*, what we *do* is also pretty important—even if the message it conveys is different.

How frustratingly confusing!

As a conscientious person who wants to make sure to communicate clearly, how do you strike a balance between the security of clarity and the discomfort of being direct? How do you know when you should be paying attention to body language vs. listening to what someone is saying? Is there one rule that holds true in any situation?

Unfortunately, I don't really think there *is* a simple answer. My rule in my own interactions tends to be to ask directly if I notice body language that seems uncomfortable or if there is a big intimacy jump in what I'm doing with someone else. Now, I have to mention, both of those things are completely relative and will vary from person to person, so it's not a perfect system. I try to listen to what someone is saying (is this an excited "yes!," a reluctant "yes…," a questioning "yes?") while also keeping an ear out for their tone of voice and an eye on their body language. Are they closing off their body? Are they smiling with their eyes as well as their mouth? Are they leaning in or away? I also listen to my own gut. How do I feel about the situation?

While this comes up in classes I teach most often around sexuality, it's also true in friendships.

My roommate, for example, works long and physically exhausting days. When she gets home, she's often the first person I've seen all day, especially when I'm writing! So I feel eager to share with her the things that happened that day. But as I'm aware that she just got home, I see what her body language is like before I say anything—is she hunched over? Does she seem energetic? When I greet her, does she respond with a "hi!" or a "hey..."? I've also taught myself to make sure the first question out of my mouth is "How was your day?" and I listen and respond to her answer. Then, before I volunteer the things I want to say, I ask her, "Can I tell you about some drama that happened on TikTok today?" or whatever the thing is. It doesn't take much time to do, but she feels a lot better knowing that she isn't going to be overwhelmed as soon as she walks in the door, and I feel better knowing that she's got the space to listen.

The fact is, some people are going to find that you asking directly what they like and what they want shatters the illusion of mind reading and "romance," or they'll feel that telling you directly what they want is "work." We are discouraged so often from being honest and blunt (while polite!) about how we feel and what we think, so it's not surprising that this tendency trickles into our intimate times. Personally, I choose to minimize the risk of miscommunication, even if that feels like a turnoff to someone else. But that line is really different for everyone, and I don't think it's clear-cut...as much as we'd like it to be.

What are some nonverbal signs you would consider good reasons to check in with another person?

What are some verbal cues that might make you want to slow down and talk about things?

Can you think of a couple of examples of situations where you might take a pause? How would you ask to do that?

How does thinking about saying, "Hey, can we stop and have a conversation?" make you feel?

What are some ways you might be able to nonverbally and verbally encourage someone you're with to feel OK asking for a check in?

IS IT NONCONSENSUAL IF THE OTHER PERSON SAYS YES BUT DOESN'T MEAN IT?

I THINK IN ORDER TO ANSWER THIS INCREDIBLY DIFFICULT and solid question, I want to encourage you to think about it in both an abstract, philosophical way, and in a grounded, practical sort of way. The reason I think that's helpful is because I think this is where the philosophical arguments that "yes means yes" and "no means no" kind of fall apart in a real-world context. In an ideal world, everyone would feel perfectly empowered to say "yes" or "no"; they'd be comfortable with their answer, and its possible consequences would not influence their decision; and they would not feel pressured by their peers, their upbringing or society at large…but that's just not the reality.

To address this question, I kind of want to turn it around and first ask: why might you say "yes" in a situation when you mean "no"?

From my years of working with folks around these issues, it's clear a lot of us say "yes" when we want to say "I'd rather not," or "maybe, but not right now," or even a resounding "no." We say "yes" because we want to be nice, because we want to please someone, because we don't want to disappoint, because we feel obligated, because we're afraid of conflict and this feels easier. Sometimes that pressure comes directly and purposefully from the person we're saying "yes" to, something we call "coercion."

However, annoyingly, sometimes that pressure comes from our own minds and environment. If we grew up in a house where we learned that saying "no" led to some kind of punishment (yelling, maybe, or the cold shoulder), we may have a reluctance to say "no" that has been deeply rooted in us. Unpacking why we feel inclined to say "yes," especially when our body is giving us signals that we're uncomfortable (anxiety, cold sweats, upset stomach, etc.), will help us assess whether we're saying "yes" wholeheartedly.

Many times, we want to answer this question around nonconsent because on some level we want to know whose responsibility it is that a boundary was crossed. If someone says "yes" because they are threatened, then we can say the person threatening them is accountable. That feels pretty clear-cut. But if someone says "yes" because they have inner conflict that the other person doesn't know about, whose responsibility is that? Whose responsibility is it if someone says and *means* "yes" in the moment, and then has time to reconsider and wishes they had said "no"?

Many academics and educators disagree about who should take "the blame" when it comes to these kinds of situations. Personally, I try to think less in terms of who is "at fault," and who deserves to be punished or shamed, and more in terms of how we can help everyone involved feel taken care of, and how we can work to prevent this situation from happening again. While yes, there are definitely some crappy people in the world who don't care about hurting others, I find that most of the time these miscommunications happen because of unspoken and even unrealized assumptions and expectations that we have developed by observing others and from our own lived experience. It is hard to identify when it's a mistake in good faith, and when it isn't—ultimately, you will have to learn to trust your gut.

So, back to the question, is it nonconsensual if the other person says yes but doesn't mean it? The answer is…sometimes? It's really hard to say, and there's no guaranteed formula that will give you the right answer every time. It's really conditional on the context. And I know that's not the most reassuring thing to hear.

But I also think there is something freeing about allowing for a more fluid understanding of consent, one that is constantly being informed by what we know about ourselves and our place in the world. Having grace for ourselves, and grace for other people, and realizing that we're all trying the best we can with the information we have, allows us to think back and realize that we wish we hadn't said "yes" to something we said "yes" to, without there needing to be blame assigned. We can offer each other the best possible opportunity to say "no," and demonstrate that "no" will be honored and respected, while also acknowledging that we're only human and we're constantly learning.

Because I know how complicated this kind of situation can be, especially when you're the one who said "yes" initially and are now wishing you hadn't, I wrote out a more detailed example of how to handle this scenario in the Boundary Toolbox later in this book. Hopefully that can help you figure out what you would do in a similar situation before you get there…or what to do next if it has already happened.

I think the most important thing to remember is that the only person you have control over is yourself. The best thing you can do, really, is spend some time figuring out what you do and don't want so you can communicate your "yes" and "no" as upfront as possible, while also being gracious when someone says "no" to you. Do the best you can with the information you're given, both for yourself and for others. And if you feel unsure that the other person's "yes" is a true "yes," ask them open-ended questions about it; let them share with you how they feel and what they want!

Can you think of a time that you said "yes" to something and didn't mean it?

Why do you think you said "yes" in that situation, and what would have needed to happen for you to feel OK saying "no"?

How would you feel if someone said "yes" to you and later you found out they didn't mean it?

What are some ways you can make it comfortable for someone to say "no" to you instead?

How can you respond positively when someone says that they changed their mind?

WHAT'S THE BEST WAY TO TELL SOMEONE YOU'VE CHANGED YOUR MIND?

IT CAN FEEL DIFFICULT TO SPEAK UP AND SAY THAT YOUR initial "yes" has turned into a "no," especially when you're already in the midst of an activity. We might feel obligated to follow through with what we said "yes" to, we might feel uncomfortable about saying anything, we might be worried that the other person won't respect our "no." This difficulty feels especially likely when it comes to a sexual encounter—I think horny people have probably been bemoaning the potential health hazards they'll suffer if they don't follow through with sex once they're aroused for as long as humans have been able to speak! But just to be super clear: that's not true, and they'll be just fine. You can withdraw consent whenever you want to—whether they finish the job themselves or not, they'll be OK without your participation. Promise.

While there are plenty of jokes and media depictions of these kinds of sexual scenarios, something similar can also happen in social situations. Let's say you agree to host a birthday party for a friend at your house, with a small guest list of people you know. Now, let's say that friend decides to invite twice the number of people you agreed to, including some you don't get along with. You might feel your initial "yes" is now a "no," but you don't want to disappoint your friend! Whether you've changed your mind because of new information, or just because you don't want to anymore, you're absolutely allowed to.

In my experience, it feels awkward to change your mind. Our culture doesn't really respect that how we feel about something might shift over time, and tells us to grit our teeth and carry on anyway. But I like to say, "If I can't say no, then my yes doesn't mean anything," to remind myself that my ability to say no is part of what makes my consent freely given. As we talked about in the previous chapter, people can feel pressured to say "yes" when they don't mean it for a myriad of reasons, both external and internal, which is why checking in and rewarding people for advocating for themselves by saying "no" is so important!

So what are some good ways to tell someone you've changed your mind? For starters, it can depend on the dynamic and what's going on. I usually try to give the other person the ability to save some face while being direct and polite about my change in wants and needs. I might say, "Let's take a break" if I am unsure how I'm feeling and need a moment for my thoughts, or redirect back to something I feel better about by saying, "Let's go back to this instead." I might say, "Instead of this, what if we tried that?" if I'm generally enjoying the vibes but not this particular activity. All of these options leave some space for us to continue interacting, but offer some gentle direction away from what I have changed my mind around and toward something else.

Another helpful thing to explore in a more big-picture way is talking about what you're both hoping for from the interaction or agreement *before* you need to change your mind (whether it's sex, or a date, or a party, or a school project). If you want to go on a date where we watch an action movie and then get ice cream, and I want to go on a date where we go to a planetarium and then have curly fries, those may seem like really disparate wants. But perhaps we can compromise on a sci-fi action film with a stop at a diner that has good sundaes *and* curly fries? Or maybe we do your thing this week, and my thing next week? By knowing about the desire at the core of our wants, we can come up with multiple solutions that have a better chance of pleasing everyone.

But what if I am no longer enjoying the vibes? Or if I realize that I said "yes" to something and I'm now regretting it? Personally, I'm usually kind and firm. If it's a situation involving physical touch, I will move their hand off of me and physically move away from them while saying, "No thanks, I've had enough." Making sure my body language and my words are speaking the same language helps ensure that there will be no misunderstanding, around both my "no" and their reaction to hearing it.

And here's the thing. You can apologize to soften the "no" if you want, saying something like "I'm sorry, I'm just not feeling this," or by smiling and saying, "Thanks, but I've changed my mind." That allows the other person to save some face, and it may feel easier in the moment. But, and I cannot stress this enough, *you do not have to apologize*. You don't have to explain or justify why you're saying "no" if you don't want to. You get to change your mind and say so, whenever, no matter what.

Whether the other person in the interaction is a friend, or a partner, or someone you're working with on a project at school, how they react to you changing your mind is useful information. They shouldn't try to pressure you, they shouldn't keep going anyway and they shouldn't make you feel guilty. And you should remember that for your reactions, too! You don't want to push someone into doing something they don't want to do by pouting about their "no." While being told "no" can feel like rejection, and it can be hard to hear, saying "no" indicates a trust that the "no" will be respected and honored. It's a good thing! When someone says it to me, I like to say "OK! Thank you for taking care of yourself," which I know sounds cheesy as hell but it really shifts the dynamic of tension in those moments. We both leave the situation feeling better.

Advocating for your boundaries, especially when you've changed your mind or you feel what's going on is beyond the limits you agreed to, is a hard muscle to exercise! Trust me, a lot of adults struggle with these kinds of boundaries. The more you keep at it, though, the easier it becomes, and by being a role model in how you handle consent, you can help those around you pick up some best practices just through watching you.

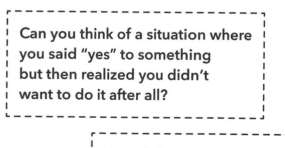

Can you think of a situation where you said "yes" to something but then realized you didn't want to do it after all?

How did you communicate that in the moment? How did it make you feel?

Can you think of some ways you could phrase your feelings if a similar situation happened?

Is there a time that someone made you feel good about saying that you changed your mind? How did their reaction impact how you felt about vocalizing your needs?

WHAT'S THE DIFFERENCE BETWEEN COERCION AND CONSENT?

COERCION SOUNDS REALLY SCARY AND INTENSE, DOESN'T it? It's usually brought up in relation to violence of some kind, and coercion can certainly have violent aspects; threats, guilt, shame, pressure and force are all examples of ways someone can get you to say "yes" when you don't feel it. It's that feeling of "if I don't say 'yes,' there will be consequences." Coercion can be explicit—when someone says something like "if you don't say 'yes,' I'll make you wish you had"—or implicit—if someone offers to drive you home from a party and then tries to kiss you without asking, you might worry about your safety. Both are types of coercion, and both are pretty shitty.

Sometimes it can be really obvious when someone is being manipulative and using coercion. But other times, especially if there is some sexual tension or interest, or if you already have a relationship with them, it can be harder to identify in the moment. People with prior relationships tend to be more likely to use negative persuasion to get their way—threatening a breakup, for example—while people who haven't been in a relationship but want to be may try to sweet-talk their way past someone's boundaries. It can be a lot harder to identify these behaviors if sex is or has been on the table. We tend to second-guess ourselves a lot!

Consent, meanwhile, ideally means saying "yes" without reservation, with our whole chest. Coercion occurs when we're saying "yes" in order to placate. In the last chapter, I mentioned a phrase I love: "If I can't say no, my yes doesn't mean anything." It reminds me that if I feel like I'm only saying "yes" to people-please or smooth something over, that's pretty likely to be coercion, not consent.

Here's where it gets tricky, though, right? Not everyone who engages in coercion is doing so consciously or maliciously. I think a lot about being out with my friends and telling them that I'm gonna head home, only for them to beg me to stay for one more round of a game, five more songs, 10 more minutes. They're not trying to make me feel bad or guilty about my boundaries! Just the opposite—they're trying to tell me indirectly that they like spending time with me and want to continue to do so, which is great, but sometimes I've got to go to sleep or I can't get up in the morning! This is an often socially acceptable type of coercion, part of the weird and nuanced dance we do in communicating with each other.

And yet, coercion between friends can also become really toxic. I was a coercive friend for years, and I didn't even really think about it. I was a queer Goth kid with a clique of other Goths and nerds, and I was often the ringleader in our group. I had two best friends, and I was frankly really mean to one of them. I would dismiss her ideas, I would tell her who I thought she should date, I never wanted to do the things she wanted to do and would label them stupid or boring without thinking. It took me years to realize that I was actually being a bully to someone I really liked, and I was very lucky that I was able to get in touch with her to apologize for how reckless I was with her boundaries. If you had asked me at the time, I would've said that I just wanted what was best for her, but that wasn't really true. I liked having control, and it made me feel good, so I coerced her into doing whatever I wanted. I wasn't thinking about making her feel bad, but when I look back, I realize I wasn't thinking of her at all. I was being a shitty friend.

I learned from my mistakes, though. I took ownership for the ways in which I had been selfish, and I learned how to check in more, how to read body language, and how to leave space in conversations for others. I learned how to compromise. I learned how to appreciate someone's enthusiasm for something even if I didn't care for it myself. I still have to check myself sometimes, too! Our society encourages coercion quite a lot and treats it as inevitable, and it's a hard thing to unlearn. But by recognizing what it can look like, both explicitly and implicitly, we can begin to notice when it's happening to us and when we're doing it to someone else, so we can pull back, apologize and do better.

To make matters even more complicated, I realized as an adult that there were times I felt like I had coerced myself into situations, or an amorphous social construct had coerced me into decisions. No external pressures *directly* influenced or threatened me. I had told myself I had to do this or I couldn't say "no" to that because there would be some sort of negative reaction…but that came from a place of anxiety, not reality. Now, the definition of coercion necessitates an "other" to do the coercing, so there is an argument that you can't coerce yourself because there's no "other." I don't want to get *too* lost in the weeds here, as self-coercion and "do we really ever have free will?" is a whole conversation you can explore in philosophy classes! I mention it here because I think it's an interesting thing to contemplate when figuring out our own will. If it's of interest to you, I'd recommend watching the TV show *The Good Place*, which talks a lot about this topic and various philosophers' approaches in an accessible, entry-point way that's also just a really fun story.

So, in short, what is the difference between coercion and consent? I guess in the simplest terms, it would be if you felt free and safe saying no. It can be messier than that, but that's a good place to start.

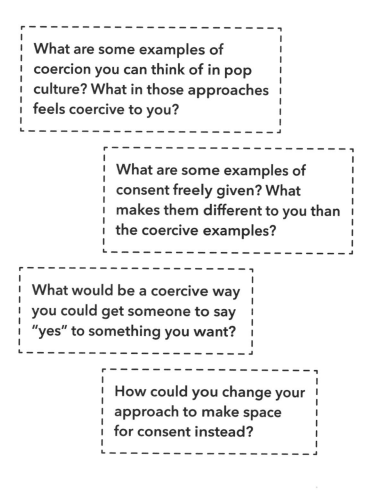

What are some examples of coercion you can think of in pop culture? What in those approaches feels coercive to you?

What are some examples of consent freely given? What makes them different to you than the coercive examples?

What would be a coercive way you could get someone to say "yes" to something you want?

How could you change your approach to make space for consent instead?

WHAT SHOULD YOU DO IF SOMEONE DOESN'T RESPECT YOUR BOUNDARIES?

WE'VE TALKED A BIT ABOUT THE WAYS THAT SOMEONE may be coercive or otherwise cross a boundary without understanding that's what they're doing, but what should you do when you see this happening in an interaction you're having? How do you put your foot down without becoming the bad guy? Must you always become the bad guy in these situations?

One thing that I've found really helpful in my own life is pulling away from the need to label people as "good guys" and "bad guys." Instead, I think about the behaviors, which makes it a little less personal. Sometimes, addressing the behavior as rude, while recognizing that the person probably isn't *trying* to be rude, allows both parties to save face while also making the boundary clear.

I have a best friend, who I absolutely love to bits, but who used to be on her phone a *lot* when we hung out. Part of that was because she's an incredibly social person (like a social hummingbird, even faster than a butterfly!), part of it was because she's really busy with responsibilities and is often juggling 10 things, and part of it was because she lives in a city where that kind of being "on" all the time is really normalized. I, on the other hand, really hated it. It made me feel ignored, especially when I had traveled to hang out with her.

So I got up some courage and told her, "Hey, when we're hanging out and you're constantly checking your phone, it feels like you're not really present with me. I know this is part of how you live a lot of the time, and I don't want you to feel bad about that—but maybe we can adjust so that there is some no-distractions, just-us time?" She was totally surprised and apologetic—she wasn't purposefully shunning me, she was just so used to doing it, she didn't even realize! We figured out a couple of times where we'd put the phones away and focus on each other, and also built into our visits some time where she could flit around setting up plans and introducing me to people. We both got what we wanted, I got my boundary respected and no one was upset.

Now, that's all well and good when someone is willing to hear your boundary and follow through, but what should you do if someone doesn't respect your boundaries? What if she had snapped at me,

"This is just how I am—deal with it" or something? Not everyone is ready and willing to self-interrogate their behavior, and some people see any attempt to assert oneself as a ploy for control. Should you just ditch anyone who doesn't respect your boundaries?

If my friend had scoffed at me or shrugged off my hurt feelings, I probably would have done a few things. I would have found something else to do in the moment. I would've privately journaled a bit about how I felt and why, so I could read it back later and see how I felt about it when I wasn't directly in the situation anymore. And I probably would've tried one more time to bring it up with her once I was back home, on the phone or via text, to see if a little distance helped. If it didn't, I probably would've chalked it up to us growing apart, and would have taken a step back. It would've stung, but I would have felt better spending more of my time with people who enjoyed quality time the way I did. Thankfully, none of that was necessary, but I've definitely had to take space from people in similar situations before!

It depends on the person, and the boundary. How much trust has built up between you? How entwined is this person with your life? How vital is this boundary to your health and well-being? Interacting with other people often means going through a period of adjustment to hearing and responding to each other's boundaries, so I typically take a moment to reflect. Is the boundary crossing something I'm willing to accept a certain amount of as we learn? Is the boundary flexible or negotiable to something that works for both parties, or is it important enough to me that I really need it to be respected as is? Remember that a real compromise means something that works for both people, not you abandoning your needs or controlling someone else!

If the boundary needs to stand, and the other person will not respect it for whatever reason, I often gently and over time detach from that person. I don't offer advice; I don't make a point of spending time together. If they try to scoop me into an argument, I politely decline to participate and I take space (whether by physically leaving, or by leaving them on read). Access to you is a privilege, not a right, and you can decide that someone's behavior is bad enough that you won't engage with them.

As I know people grow and change, I made a personal rule that I won't engage until they offer a real apology that shows they understand that they violated my boundary. This works in two ways: it makes it clear that my time and energy are limited and I won't spend it on people who are disrespectful to me, but it also demonstrates that it's about the behavior, not the person. Whether that approach is helpful for you or not, well, that's for you to figure out!

Sometimes the way someone behaves is bad enough that you can't handle being around them even if they do apologize—maybe they've demonstrated a pattern of shitty actions, or you didn't like them much to begin with. You don't owe anyone your attention, and you don't have to have a relationship with people who make you feel bad about yourself. If their behavior consistently makes you feel anxious, unsure of yourself, angry, confused or hurt, you may well be better off without them. Sometimes it's worthwhile to try and fix things, and sometimes it isn't. Trust me, you'll make plenty of mistakes in both categories during your life! That's OK, and very human.

Now, all this advice is for situations where someone is being disrespectful of your boundaries, but not escalating to something like abuse. If you think you might be experiencing something like an abusive relationship, whether it's romantic, familial, at a workplace or something else, I highly recommend you check out Scarleteen's list of resources and information about abuse. The Resources section in the back of this book also includes websites, phone lines and forums to help you figure out if the situation you're in is just shitty, or if it's abusive.

In summary? You deserve to have boundaries, and people should respect them. If someone isn't respecting your boundaries, you can address that in different ways, from more friendly to less so. Do what feels right for you *and* gets your boundaries met.

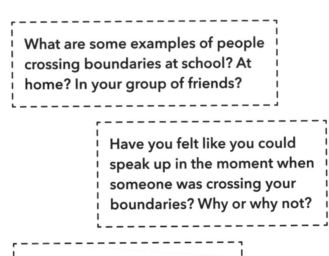

What are some examples of people crossing boundaries at school? At home? In your group of friends?

Have you felt like you could speak up in the moment when someone was crossing your boundaries? Why or why not?

What are a few phrases you could have on hand to assert your boundaries in the future?

What are some ways you might feel comfortable disengaging?

WHAT SHOULD I DO WHEN I'VE CROSSED SOMEONE'S BOUNDARIES?

WHEN I FIRST STARTED DOING WORK AROUND CONSENT culture, the focus was mostly on supporting people whose boundaries had been crossed. It was understandable, since we still live in a culture where people get blamed in court for "tempting fate" with their clothes or behavior, which is absurd. Educating people on how to take care of themselves and the people around them in those situations *is* really important, and this education is still chronically lacking, particularly when it comes to teenagers.

However, there is another part of this equation that I think is also incredibly important and even *less* often discussed. What should you do when you're the one who fucked up? Does it mean you're now a horrible person who should be shunned from society? Are you unsafe to be around?

The painful truth that many people don't want to acknowledge, I think, is that we cross each other's boundaries and lines all the time. It's really hard to talk about because sometimes, we don't know something is a boundary until the train has left the station, and we certainly aren't born knowing all of our boundaries. Hell, our boundaries change as we change!

Now, clearly, there is a difference between someone who is predatory and looking for opportunities to violate consent and control other people, and someone who stepped on someone else's foot accidentally and will try very hard to avoid doing it again. One of the ways I've learned to assess whether a person is holding themselves accountable for fucking up or not is to see how they react when they're told about it—and another is if it happens again.

This is also true for assessing my own reactions, and that was a hard pill to swallow at first.

It took an embarrassingly long time to reprogram myself out of being defensive when someone told me I had hurt them in some way. I didn't mean to, I'd say, or I didn't know that what I did was hurtful—as if that took away the effects of my actions or gave solace to the person I affected. Sometimes I found ways to directly or indirectly blame the other person for their feelings, like it was a communication issue on their part, or they took what I did too personally.

It took a lot of introspection and humility, but now I understand that my knee-jerk reaction to being told I hurt someone is feeling guilty and ashamed, and that my defensiveness is a natural self-protection response. That said, just because something comes to us automatically doesn't mean that it's the right thing to do. I have absolutely kicked a table leg after stubbing my toe on it because striking out was my automatic response to the pain. It didn't help matters. My toe was just twice stubbed!

Eventually, I realized that it was perhaps in my best interest to explore my reactions and see if they were actually useful to me or standing in my way. I also realize now that when someone offers me feedback or criticism about my behavior, I don't have to receive it as an attack. Our society tends to make these situations combative, as if you're automatically in conflict because one of you was hurt by the other, but it can also be a place for apology and healing, instead of pouring salt on the wound.

Now, when someone tells me I hurt them, I can feel the anxiety pang in my stomach and the flush of shame in my cheeks, and I can stop myself. I can breathe through it, remind myself that I am not in danger and that I don't need to be hypervigilant, that this person is telling me this so that I can improve myself and thus not hurt people in the future, which is a gift. I can stay calm and apologize for my fuckup, and I can ask what I can do to fix it, if I can fix it.

Later, I can reflect on the situation further—I can consider the context in which the feedback was given, my history with that person and if I can see where they were coming from. And I'll be honest—sometimes, I genuinely can't. After all, not all feedback is given in good faith (I remember school as being a place rife with drama and rumors!). That said, if I don't react defensively, if I choose to react as if the feedback is being given in good faith and receive it as such, it will empower a person who really is hurt and will disempower someone trying to get a reaction out of me. Either way, the result is better than a defensive response would have gotten.

The last thing I'll add here is that different people appreciate different kinds of apologies. Saying "I'm sorry" is important to some people, and seeing that someone is sorry through their deeds (making it up to them) is important to others. I've definitely put my foot in it giving an explanation to someone as part of an apology when they didn't care *why* it happened, just *that* it happened! Usually, my format is to acknowledge what I did wrong, what I should have done instead and what I'll do better next time, unless I know that this person really likes being asked for forgiveness or something else that's not addressed in my normal apology.

"What can I do to help you feel safe/seen in this moment?" can also be a good addition to an apology. Sometimes, the answer will be to give them space—definitely do that, if they ask, and let them come to you when they're ready. That gives the power back to them, for them to choose how to engage and when. We're often given examples in media of throwing apologies at someone we hurt over and over until they forgive us—but that's just another assault on their boundaries! When we let the ball be in their court, they will usually feel less pestered and have the time they need to feel what they need to feel about what happened.

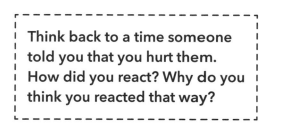

Think back to a time someone told you that you hurt them. How did you react? Why do you think you reacted that way?

After working through some of the questions and reading some of the stories in this book, how would you like to react now?

What are some ways you can check in with yourself to be more present and open to feedback?

WHEN IS A BOUNDARY HEALTHY?
CAN BOUNDARIES BE DETRIMENTAL?

ONE THING I THINK WE REALLY BEGIN TO WRANGLE WITH as we transition from children to adults is a more complex understanding of boundaries. Initially, we may understand boundaries as walls that separate us and others, sometimes with the intention of protecting us, and sometimes with the intention of keeping other people away. They're the space between where "you"–your physical self ("I don't want to be hugged right now") and your emotional self ("I'm not able to have this conversation today")–end and another person begins. At least, that's a very simplistic understanding of boundaries.

But a boundary can also exist in a behavioral sense, like around how you want people to interact with you. When you're doing your homework, for example, you might set a nonverbal boundary by silencing the ringer on your phone so you don't get distracted. Or it might be something you set with a friend who loves to share gossip: "I don't want to hear speculation about so-and-so's relationship status." Boundaries can be situational ("I'll tell you about my crush when I feel ready") or long-standing ("I'm not interested in smoking—please stop asking me"). I think of stating boundaries as being a way I can communicate and control my own behavior, without trying to control the behavior of those around me.

While many people focus on boundaries in romantic or sexual relationships, they also absolutely exist in other situations! You may have boundaries with your siblings about when you want time to yourself, or with your friends about a topic you don't like being teased about. In fact, I'm a firm believer that the more we practice healthy boundaries in other areas of our lives, the more likely we'll have healthy boundaries in our romantic and sexual lives. Setting boundaries is like working out to strengthen a muscle—as you do it more, it becomes a lot easier.

So what is a healthy boundary? I think people will define it differently for themselves, so I want to encourage you to think about what makes a boundary feel healthy or unhealthy for you. For me, a healthy boundary is ideally one that works to keep me physically and emotionally safe while not controlling or manipulating another person. It doesn't necessarily mean I'll always be *comfortable*—if someone tells me something I said is racist, for example, that will be *uncomfortable*—but I'm still *safe* at the end of the day.

Also, a healthy boundary is one where I can advocate for my wants and needs without infringing on someone else's wants and needs, which of course means I have to know what my wants and needs are! This kind of self-knowledge helps me determine when someone is close to crossing a boundary, often before it happens, so I can vocalize that and alert the other person that they're getting close to a line. It also means that if the person decides to move ahead anyway, I have already told them the consequences of how I will behave in response to their actions.

Wow, you might think, that sounds really positive! How can boundaries possibly be detrimental? Well, first of all, setting boundaries is an imperfect process that usually takes some trial and error to strike the right balance. I know I have to be careful that I'm not declaring a boundary because I'm afraid of being uncomfortable, or because I'm afraid of being alone. In an attempt to protect myself, I have a tendency to be a little too rigid with my boundaries, and over the years I've learned to be a little more flexible while still not being a pushover. It's a dynamic process that I'll probably be mastering my whole life!

Unhealthy boundaries could end up being ones that are too flexible, where you find yourself trying to people-please to your own detriment by denying your experiences or not saying "no." Or (like what I'm unlearning), unhealthy boundaries could be too rigid, immediately shutting people out when things feel complicated or vulnerable out of fear of being hurt. Finally, boundaries can be unhealthy when they're weaponized to punish someone—"If you don't do exactly what I tell you, I'll break up with you." Often a weaponized boundary is used as a threat to manipulate the other person's behavior; whether or not they follow through with it, the implied punishment is the point.

Where this distinction between healthy and unhealthy boundaries gets complicated is when the other person's behavior harms you and your sense of autonomy and well-being. One person's healthy boundary can be perceived by another as an unhealthy ultimatum. "If you lie to me again, I'm going to dump you" is probably a healthy boundary, except for when it's not (like, for example, if that person insists they aren't lying, and you're punishing them out of anxiety). Or you might say to a friend, "Hey, I want to be available to support you during your breakup, but I need to focus on homework for the next hour." Figuring out how to communicate boundaries in a way that shows compassion for yourself and for those around you ends up being a deeply individual and constantly shifting process! It's OK for there to be a learning curve.

How you establish a healthy boundary with people who have earned your trust vs. people you don't really know, or with people you can choose to not engage with (a classmate, say) vs. people you don't have much choice about engaging with (like a family member) is going to vary. At the end of the day, the challenge is to set boundaries in a way that doesn't seek to control others, while also drawing a line about what you will and will not put up with.

> **How do you define a boundary for yourself?**

> **What boundaries do you have for yourself with other people? How do those boundaries serve you?**

> **Did any past hurts contribute to these boundaries? Who is a person in your life who respects your boundaries, and how do their actions show you they respect them?**

CONSENT AND AUTHORITY:
HOW DO YOU PICK YOUR BATTLES?

THIS SECTION ASSUMES A NON-ABUSIVE DYNAMIC between caregivers and teens, but it's important to note that general statistics make it clear that a lot of youth are in abusive or neglectful situations—worldwide, some studies say it's one in four, while others say it's one in three. Regardless of how many, it's too many. If you think you might be one of them, the resources in the back of this book can offer some guidance, particularly Scarleteen, which has a phone line, message boards, live chat and text chat. Since these situations are often so individual, it's hard to offer the right advice, as what's great for one person may be harmful for another. But you don't have to figure this out alone—please reach out to folks who can help you figure out next steps!

I am very lucky in that I was raised in a household with anarchist parents who cared deeply about teaching me about autonomy. They made sure I learned from an early age that adults were not necessarily trustworthy, and that questioning authority was good, actually. I think they expected me to do that in relation to my teachers at school more so than in relation to them, my parents, and I suspect there were times they regretted having encouraged me to push back so hard—but in general, they gave me really solid tools to think critically about things I was told, and they taught me to research claims and to challenge ideas that went against my morals. While I'm sure it made parenting more difficult for them in many ways, it did protect me from a lot of potential harm.

There will come a time when you look at your caregivers and realize that while they are authority figures in your life, charged with your well-being and hopefully keeping you safe and healthy, they are also…well, people. They're humans with their own upbringings and biases, their own fears and experiences and dreams. They're perfectly capable of messing up and having bad days (not that something being understandable makes it justifiable!). Being an adult does not inherently mean that you have done a lot of self-exploration. Many adults are just learning about the intricacies and nuances of consent themselves, and it's blowing their minds.

Fortunately, reading this book hopefully means you will be better prepared than many people who have never considered the questions posed in the chapter titles; you can go out into the world knowing more about what you want and how to ask for it! Unfortunately, you are probably still living at home, and therefore are navigating your increasing freedoms and independence while also having to follow certain household rules. The adults you interact with may not have as much of an awareness of consent as you now have, and it can be difficult to explain these concepts to them in a way that they're able to hear. That can be incredibly frustrating. You may find yourself straining against guidelines and demands that you feel are unreasonable and don't make sense to you. This uncomfortable dance is part of being a teen, and it's part of being a caregiver to a teen.

When I was researching for this chapter, I found it really telling that looking up "boundaries for teenagers" gave me results focused entirely on teenagers having boundaries with their peers, and not with how to communicate boundaries with the adults in their lives. Yet it's something teens have to deal with all the time. Maybe you have to tell your parents not to joke about your crushes or your body because it makes you feel uncomfortable. Maybe you're figuring out how to ask questions around sex, gender, sexual orientation or birth control, without getting into too-much-information territory. Maybe you just need some private time that stays private! That's all super valid. You get to have boundaries, including with the adults in your life.

That said, it's important to remember to humanize your caregivers, especially if they raised you from the time you were a small child. It can be difficult for a caregiver to recognize that their "little baby is growing up," and it can take a little time for them to catch up. That doesn't mean they should infantilize you—not only is that kinda irritating, but it's also not preparing you for the world—but I think it's possible sometimes to roll your eyes and remember that they are still just people, at the end of the day, and they're figuring this stuff out too.

There is something to be said for picking your battles when it comes to getting your caregivers to hear you in relation to your boundaries or what you want. It's not because you don't deserve to have those boundaries and wants respected and heard—you absolutely do! But they are also likely unlearning some unhealthy norms around consent and autonomy, and if you try to challenge them in multiple ways at once, many adults will get defensive and just shut down. That doesn't get your needs met—it just upsets everyone, including you!

When I was a young adult, I learned that if I vocally advocated for myself against rules that *really* mattered to me, but I respected the rest of them, I was more likely to find success. Because my caregivers knew that I wasn't just fighting them on everything, all the time, they tended to listen more readily when I put my foot down. This was also a great way to foster trust between us, as they trusted that I wasn't going to sneak behind their backs while lying to them. I learned to be upfront about what I felt didn't give me the autonomy I had earned, and they were more inclined to grant me the independence I requested.

Now, of course this advice comes with a caveat—not all caregivers are reasonable, and not all are willing to negotiate. Sometimes you just have to work with what you're given. But I've found that more often than not, if you approach the conversation in good faith and have a well-considered argument, with perhaps a compromise of your own to offer, you'll be surprised at what you can achieve. For example, maybe you usually can't go out to the movies on a school night, but it's a friend's birthday; you might be able to persuade your caregivers to let you go this once, and you'll pick up an extra chore over the weekend. They might still say no, but they might say yes, and it's worth asking! You won't always get what you want, but it's still good practice (just be sure to respect *their* "no," too!). And of course, sometimes you'll have to "lose a battle so you can win the war" over the long term—give up on the instant gratification of staying up late to watch a show you like today so that you can stay out late for a concert down the line—and that's also OK.

All that said…battles with authority can be a goddamn mess. Between you and me, I had some rough times with my caregivers growing up. I loved them, but I was also angry with them a lot, and some of the choices they made about how they managed their mental health and their lives were not especially healthy for me. That was incredibly hard during a period where I was expected to respect the authority of my parents and follow their rules. I would see them yelling, my mother storming off, doors slamming, manipulation—not the best lessons in how to handle conflict.

I was a Bad Kid in many ways: I fought with my parents all the time, I ran away from home, I lied to them, all kinds of stuff. I hated doing my homework and slept during class. I thought I was the problem, and I didn't really care what the consequences would be. I didn't feel connected to my parents at all. There was a time when I thought we might not ever feel like a safe and loving family for me, and I had to come to terms with that. It was hard. Really hard. And it felt very isolating and scary.

But here's what I learned (and maybe this will be relatable, or maybe not): my parents were just people at the end of the day. Yeah, they made some bad decisions. They even made some selfish decisions. They weren't always the most supportive and emotionally available. In our case, I moved across the country, from Massachusetts to California, and rebuilt my life somewhere completely new. I went to therapy. I did a lot of introspection (sometimes with the guided assistance of psilocybin, not gonna lie). And slowly, over time, my parents and I have become actual, genuine friends. We built up a relationship again, learning to trust each other through clear expectations and communicated boundaries. With work from both sides, we were able to heal rifts I thought would be unfixable. But I couldn't fix it alone; I needed some time to sort out my own head and they needed some space to realize that they were also contributing to the strife. Sometimes distance really does make the heart grow fonder. It certainly helps give us perspective, including on whether this is a healthy and positive relationship or if it's maybe a relationship we're happier without.

What are some rules you have in your household that you wish you could live without?

What are some ways you could offer a compromise that might change the minds of your caregivers?

How can you present that compromise in a way that respects your caregivers' rules, and why they have them, while also saying why you want to do something different?

Can you think of some authorities in your life that you've had to assert boundaries with? Did you feel your boundaries were understood and respected? Why or why not?

WHAT DOES IT MEAN TO "NAVIGATE YOUR OWN CONSENT"?

I MENTIONED IN THE INTRODUCTION SOMETHING I CALLED "navigating your own consent." It's kind of a weird concept, considering we mostly talk about consent as a dynamic between two or more people. So then, what does it mean?

I put this question at the end of the book in part because I think you'll understand what I was getting at a little better now that you've gone through the other prompts. But I still wanted to outline why I think it's important to spend some time thinking about yourself in relation to consent. What do you want? What do you not want? Are any of those things conditional? What changes your mind in a way that still feels good and empowered for you?

I think when we talk about consent in relation to how we interact with others, it's all too easy to get lost in our desire to please someone, or look cool, or piss off our parents—and the underlying question of "what do *I* want, right now" can get a little muddy. By being able to tease out what I want, and what I'd like to push myself to do even if it makes me feel a little uncomfortable, and what I definitely don't want to do, I can make better, more conscious choices in the moment, because I'm more alert to my own red flags when I flip from feeling excited but nervous to dread. These emotions can sometimes feel pretty similar until you've hurtled past that line!

Here's an example from my own life, and hopefully it won't make me sound incredibly uncool.

I'm actually a pretty introverted person. I like to go to parties with friends sometimes, but they can make me feel socially anxious. For a long time, I made myself go to big parties where I had to shout to be heard, where I didn't get to have deep conversations with good friends the way I prefer but instead was making small talk with strangers. I didn't enjoy myself most of the time, but I told myself that this was what it meant to have a social life, and so I needed to suck it up and figure it out!

You would think that I would have realized that I'd be much happier having quiet tea parties and picnics, doing introvert stuff, but that's not what happened for many years. Instead, I pushed myself until I felt really awkward, and then I'd drink or smoke in order to feel like I was assimilating. I felt like I needed something in my hands so I didn't feel quite so weird. I forced myself to perform being an extrovert because I was afraid if I didn't, I would feel left out and boring. What would then happen is I'd smoke too much, or drink too much, and feel awful the next day. I'd tell myself that I wouldn't do *that* again, and in a week's time I'd have completely forgotten about how gross I felt, and I'd do the whole dance again. I did that for years, trying to mold myself into what I thought I should be, rather than stopping to examine what I actually wanted to do.

Obviously you can't anticipate every possibility you might run across in your day-to-day life. But you *can* do some groundwork to better understand what you generally like to do, and when you might push through and do something you're not as into, and what your motivations to do so might be. The only person we have 100% control over is ourselves, so knowing yourself is pretty important for having as much information as possible when navigating consent with others!

To be fair, a lot of us don't really know what we want in a deep, satisfying kind of way. What we want is often a complicated mess impacted by what we think is possible, what we think is likely, what we're willing to tolerate (and for what purpose), and what we're willing to reach for. It's also something that will change throughout your life, as you grow older and have new life experiences. That's OK! It's good to be flexible, as well as informed. I just think that spending some time thinking about what makes you feel happy and fulfilled can help you make choices that serve that goal. Then you have an idea of things that you want to say "yes" (or "no"!) to for your own reasons, not because someone wants you to or you saw someone else do it.

I think teens are often denied a certain amount of autonomy because caregivers are afraid that once they let you make choices for yourself, you'll vanish and they'll never see you again, or you'll do something reckless and harm yourself or someone else. Most of the time, they're not intentionally trying to prevent you from finding your own way. They're trying to protect you. But when they do that, they're often accidentally communicating that you should be serving their wants and needs over your own…especially when you ask them for their reasoning and they just say, "because I said so." We talked a bit about picking your battles in an earlier chapter, and your caregivers would probably be mad if I didn't mention that sometimes they have more perspective than you do, and that's why they're pushing you to make a particular decision. Sometimes, you just have to go along with what they say, as annoying as that can feel. You'll have plenty of time to make reckless decisions, don't worry—you don't need to rush!

Ultimately, consent culture is about trust, right? And trusting yourself is absolutely the core of it.

You'll need to constantly check in with yourself to figure out how to feel about this situation, at this time in your life, with these people—it's like a living document, not a one-and-done sort of thing! I'm hoping that this book has helped you gain more of that awareness without telling you how to be or what to think. That bit's up to you, now. I believe in you!

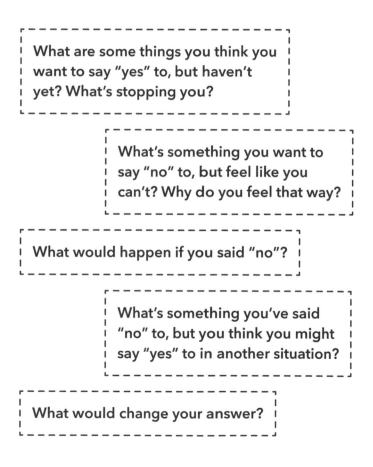

What are some things you think you want to say "yes" to, but haven't yet? What's stopping you?

What's something you want to say "no" to, but feel like you can't? Why do you feel that way?

What would happen if you said "no"?

What's something you've said "no" to, but you think you might say "yes" to in another situation?

What would change your answer?

THE BOUNDARY TOOLBOX

I KNOW THIS BOOK OFFERS A LOT OF COMPLEX IDEAS and questions, and answering them is difficult. Where do you even begin? Asking yourself when you may have experienced some of these things, and how you felt and how you might deal with them in the future, is all well and good, but sometimes it can help to have some scripts to use when you're feeling a little tongue-tied.

In this chapter, I've pulled out three significant interactions that you might experience. I've offered some examples of how you could handle each situation in a few different ways, with outlines of some things you can say or do. At the end of the day, though, I'll quote Captain Awkward, one of my favorite online advice columnists, who talks about boundaries a lot: "Maintaining boundaries isn't really about what you can persuade other people to do, it's about deciding what you are willing to do in order to get your needs met when and if someone isn't persuaded."

This is really vital to keep in mind moving forward. The only person you have control over is yourself!

The below scripts and scenarios are to help you before you get to that point. These are not going to work in every situation, and they may not even be applicable for your specific situation. But my hope is that rather than telling you *what* to do, I'm giving you guidelines on *how* to do it. Take what works for you, and leave the rest!

- -

How to Say "No" While Saving Face and Letting Others Save Face

Let's say you have a friend who likes to talk on the phone. You like this person a lot, but you also have a pretty busy life with homework, chores, after-school activities, hobbies and other friends. You've had a difficult time getting off the phone with them when you've picked up, and no amount of polite hints seems to get the message across. While you want to touch base, you really can't afford to have every phone call take over an hour! They've just called you again after school, and you're finding yourself dreading looking at the missed calls. You care about your friend, but how do you kindly let them know you can't be endlessly available?

Here are a few ways you can say "no" to your friend, both in the moment and in advance, that allow them to save some face while also letting you save face and set a boundary. No one has to be the mean guy here!

Offer an Alternative

If you want to have a long gabfest but right now just isn't the ideal time, offering an alternative is a great option. Try, "Hi friend! I have a lot on my plate today. How about we have a conversation on this other day when I'll have more time to talk?" Then make sure you prioritize chatting with this friend on that day. Don't just offer an alternative to be polite if you don't actually want to chat with them, and make sure that alternative is in fact a good time for you before you suggest it. I've also offered, "Maybe you can send me a voice memo and I'll respond when I have a bit of free time" as an alternative to immediate interaction.

Add a Qualifier

You might find it helpful to set a time limit on your attention, with a clearly defined and communicated end point. For example, "Hey friend! I have a lot on my plate today but I'd like to chat. I've set my alarm for 20 minutes, and after that I have to get on with my responsibilities." After making a statement like this, make sure to follow through—it communicates that this is a boundary you are serious about, which will help in the future when you set boundaries with this person. Personally, I use this one a lot! It allows me to touch base with my friends and show them I do care, but it also helps me not feel as stressed because I know when I'll be able to get off the phone.

Redirect

This one is a little closer to fibbing, but I've used it on occasion when I wanted to sidestep a conversation about why I'm not available. "Hey, I saw you called; I can't call you back today, I've gotta have family time" or similar works to help both of you save face—it's not that you don't *want* to, you just can't right now. Use this strategy sparingly, because when you use it too often to avoid having an honest conversation about boundaries, you can come across as flaky and/or fake.

Remember That "No" Is a Complete Sentence

You may try your best, but no amount of careful communication will lead to your friend hearing your boundary 100% of the time. In those cases, it is absolutely OK to just say, "I can't do that, no." I like to remind myself not to say, "Sorry, no" if I am not in fact sorry; I don't like to apologize as an empty gesture, and I don't want the other person to see an apology as an entry point for a negotiation. The answer can just be "no."

- -

I Consented to Something, but Now I Regret It. What Do I Do Now?

To be clear, I'm referring to a situation where you gave enthusiastic consent and later realized the situation didn't end up being worth the intimacy. This scenario isn't about a situation where you were coerced, or stayed silent, or were overpowered, or were under the influence of alcohol or drugs. This scenario is about regret, not trauma or harm! If you are experiencing or have experienced trauma or harm due to an intimate situation, please do reach out to the resources in the back of this book so you can get specialized help with your situation.

In general, I've been talking about consent in relation to many situations, not just sexual, because of course how we interact with and manage consent out of bed will impact our comfort with communicating about it in bed (or the car, or wherever else you hook up!). But I wanted to talk about consent specifically as it relates to having a sexual experience you later regret, because I think we as a society don't really talk about how often that happens. I teach about consent, and I've definitely looked back at some of my past hookup encounters and cringed, even when I was fully enthusiastic about those experiences in the moment!

Let's say you met up with someone at a party and hit it off. You were flirting heavily, the music was good, you danced together and that was fun… so you got a little handsy on the couch. But you woke up the next day thinking, "Ugh, that escalated quickly, and I don't know if I want to do it again," and now things feel complicated. You're having that feeling of, "Well, *that* wasn't my best idea…" How do you handle it from here?

Own It

Look, we all make impulsive mistakes some-times, whether it's kissing someone when we weren't really into it, or texting a nude to someone and then wishing we could take it back. How do you talk to yourself about it afterward? Do you give yourself the same grace you would give a friend who found themselves in the same situation, or do you put yourself down? You get to own the things you learned, and sometimes that road is bumpy. I know what I'm talking about—let's just say I've had a couple of experiences that weren't worth writing down—but I learned a bit about myself, and I didn't make those mistakes again (granted, I made new ones, but hey).

Ask Yourself, "What Can I Learn from This?"

When the situation is one where no one got hurt, but I feel like I regret my choices, I like to look back and think about how it happened. Sometimes I made an impulsive decision because everyone else was hooking up and I didn't want to feel left out, or sometimes I just wanted to see what kissing a particular person would be like. Sometimes you take a calculated risk and it doesn't work out! What you can do is figure out how to change your calculations so next time you look back and feel good about what you've done and why. It's not about shaming yourself, but about rolling your eyes ruefully and saying, "Welp, not doing that again."

Decide about Disclosure

Should you tell the other person how you feel? I guess the question I have for this scenario is, "What's the goal?" Am I telling the other person that I regretted hooking up or making out or whatever because I want to set a clear boundary that it won't happen again? Can I do that in a milder way—and do I want to? Is there something about the interaction that they could change and that would have made me feel better about the situation—say, did you kiss someone who had just had a bunch of pizza, so their breath was awful? If there's a little bit of advice I can offer, I might choose to do so, especially if I like the person—"Hey, next time, grab a little gum first" is a kinder way to communicate than "Your breath was godawful."

- -

I Crossed Someone's Boundary. How Do I Fix It?

Here is an awkward and uncomfortable truth: no matter how much we have educated ourselves, and how careful we are, we have probably crossed someone's boundaries before, and we will probably cross someone's boundary again in our lives. Interpersonal relationships are complicated and the intricacies take a lifetime to learn. As well-meaning as we are, we will probably misread a signal in order to receive the answer we want to hear, or we'll do something without thinking that we said we wouldn't do. Mistakes happen. Moments of cruelty, even, can happen, when we say something mean because our feelings are hurt, or we act selfishly in the moment and later regret our choices.

While it is noble to learn as much as we can to avoid harming others as best we're able, the fact is, we are gonna mess up. The real measure of our character, then, comes from how we respond to messing up. Are we defensive and closed off, or do we take ownership and some time to reflect on what we did? Do we offer a genuine apology, or a snarky "sorry you feel that way"?

Let's say your friend A told you about a crush they have on someone. A swore you to secrecy, and you promised you wouldn't breathe a word of it. But then, when talking to another friend, B, you accidentally let slip this crush of A's. B tells one of their friends, and eventually it gets back to A, who is now angry and embarrassed that you leaked their secret. What can you do now?

Admit That Sometimes, You're Wrong

Sometimes it's a misunderstanding, but sometimes you're just wrong, you blew it and you have to take the L. Learning how to be humble in these moments and acknowledge that you made a mistake is vital for helping the person whose boundaries you crossed feel heard in their pain. I call this "baring my belly"—like when a wolf shows submissiveness to another wolf by showing their belly. It's a sign of trust, saying, "You can tear into my soft guts if you want, but I trust you not to."

By baring my belly, I offer my vulnerability and my responsibility to the person I've hurt, which often leads them to not feel like they need to be on the attack.

Apologize Genuinely

Different people appreciate different things from an apology, so you may need to try a couple of strategies to see what works for the person whose boundary you crossed. In general, I think an apology should say what happened, what I did wrong, what I should have done and what I plan to do in the future to make sure this doesn't happen again. Some people might appreciate being asked how I can make it up to them, and others really need to hear the words "I'm sorry." Sometimes people want to know why you did what you did, and sometimes they don't; they just want to hear that you know you were in the wrong and are going to do better next time. The apology should be about centering them and their feelings, not about making you feel less guilty.

Learn from the Experience

Think about how and why this happened, and what you're going to do to avoid making the same mistake again. This is how we can build up trust, by walking the walk and demonstrating that we take the fact that we hurt someone seriously. Now, it's important to keep in mind that you can only control your own behavior, here—you can't make someone trust or forgive you, you can only act in such a way as to show that you have learned and grown. I find that as hard as it can be to let people have their process, even if that means being angry with me for a time, it results in stronger friendships down the line that are based in being real with each other. I think that's ultimately worth the discomfort.

A CHECKLIST OF CHECK-INS

HOW DO YOU KNOW THAT A SITUATION IS NONCONSEN-sual? It can be difficult to figure it out, especially in the moment. Sometimes we want something and we don't want it at the same time—or maybe we want the thing, but not the consequences or the aftermath! Here are some indirect, environmental or nonverbal things I look for in my interactions with people as possible red flags that would make me want to stop in my tracks and talk about what's going on.

These suggestions are intended to be initial questions you can ask yourself, rather than proof that your situation is consensual or nonconsensual. Each one is a starting place to help you be more mindful of how you feel, and how those around you may feel, but not a substitute for talking to each other. I highly recommend doing both! There are reasons why these things can happen in consensual situations—people are shy, for example, or neurodivergent—so think of these questions more as guideposts that maybe it'd be good to check in more directly.

Physical and Emotional Signs

☐ How does my gut feel? Do I feel excited, or do I feel a sense of dread?

☐ Do I feel comfortable asking for what I want?

☐ Am I getting positive body language (making eye contact, smiling, mimicking my body language like crossing my legs)?

☐ Are they expressionless or motionless?

Current Capacity

☐ Would I feel guilty if I said "no" to this ask?

☐ Am I under the influence of something that would lead me to say "yes" when I don't mean it (substances, peer pressure, a desire to please)?

☐ Is there a power imbalance here (age, position on a team, popularity)?

☐ Can I easily and safely leave this situation right now? Can they?

☐ When I ask this person for what they want, do they tell me?

☐ Have they given an enthusiastic "yes"—or are they saying "maybe," "I want to, but" or nothing?

☐ Might they be under the influence of something?

Relationship Assessment

☐ Do I think this person would act differently if I said "no" to this ask?

☐ When I have said "no" in the past, how have they reacted? How did that make me feel?

☐ Do I trust that this person will stop if I ask or tell them to stop?

☐ Am I honest with this person? Do I feel supported by them?

☐ How do they talk about friends they've fallen out with, or their exes? Do I worry they'd say things behind my back if I say "no"?

☐ How have I reacted to them saying "no" to me in the past?

☐ Would I act differently with this person if they said "no" to me now?

☐ How do I talk about friends I've fallen out with, or my exes?

It can feel weird sometimes to stop and check in. We're shown in movies and TV shows that if we care about each other or like each other, we'll somehow just "know" how we feel, and how they feel. That's definitely not true!

Remember that phrase I mentioned in the chapter about coercion? "If I can't say no, then my yes doesn't mean anything." It sounds simple, but it's really helpful in differentiating if I'm consenting, or if I feel like I have to say "yes" on some level.

TL;DR: A BRIEF LIST OF CONSENT TIPS

THESE TIPS AREN'T INTENDED TO BE ALL-INCLUSIVE, BUT rather a quick and dirty summary of some of the stuff I talk about in this book in case you want a refresher or some reassurance. That said—there's no substitute for direct communication!

- Everyone defines consent differently—asking open-ended questions and being clear about your desires and limits can help you get on the same page!
- Create space for others to respond to checking in by letting them do it in their own time and in their own words. Sometimes, we don't know what we want or like in the moment, and it's OK to take a breath to think about it!
- Consent relies on everyone having the same information (often referred to as "informed consent"). Communicating clearly and honestly, including when you're not sure or you've

changed your mind, is a good way to check for informed consent.

- Consent flourishes in environments without pressure, manipulation or mind-altering substances. However, we live in a world with pressures of all kinds, both explicit and implicit, all around us. The ideal is to recognize those pressures and strive to minimize their influence over our choices.

- Saying "yes" to something once, or under certain circumstances, doesn't mean it's a "yes" every time. See also: if someone says "yes" to making out, it's not a "yes" to taking clothes off. Ask first!

- Verbal consent is one form of consent, in which people say "yes," "no," "maybe," "not right now," etc. Nonverbal consent (body language, tone, eye contact) is also important. If someone says "yes" but they sound uncomfortable, or they won't meet your eyes? Check in, because that may not be a true "yes." It's better to stop when you hear or sense reluctance than to push ahead and cross a boundary.

- You can change your mind. People change their minds all the time! Sometimes you're feeling it, and then suddenly you aren't. That's OK! Consent is reversible.

- Stay humble—even with the best of intentions, you can still get it wrong. That's OK! It doesn't mean you're a bad person; consent is forever a practice, not a mastery. Learn from the experience, take ownership and do better next time.

- Remember that when someone says "no" to you, it may feel like a bummer, but it's also a sign that they trust you to respect their "no," which is awesome! By responding positively to "no," you are encouraging that person to feel they can trust you with their communicated boundaries.

FINAL THOUGHTS

WHEW, YOU MADE IT THROUGH THE BOOK. I KNOW IT was probably a lot of information, maybe a little confusing and maybe a little overwhelming. It's a lot for me too, sometimes, and I've been working on consent culture, what it means and how to do it, for over 13 years!

I hope this doesn't come off as condescending, but I'm proud of you for picking up this book and giving it a try. This shit is hard! A lot of adults pay lip service to the ideas in here but never dig much deeper. I hope the questions in this book gave you some things to think about, and that I was able to offer you...not rules, really, but methods to make better assessments and communicate your boundaries in a healthy but firm way. And you should question me, too, frankly! I'm just one person with my own biases and experiences. This is ultimately your life, and your path.

It was also really important to me that the language of this book was accessible and inviting. I know I can be kind of an intense person! I didn't want this book to use academic language or a bunch of citations you needed to look up. I wanted to provide resources to help guide you forward and a glossary for how I use the terms I've mentioned, but I didn't want it to feel like classwork. I hope you have found the prompts and anecdotes to be gentle, and like invitations to explore, rather than gatekeeping and alienating. I want you to leave this work feeling curious, not lectured.

I know doing the work to understand what consent and consent culture mean to you personally can be hard and humbling. Nothing has shown me how little I knew about myself and how much I assumed and took for granted about my experience being universal like talking about consent culture! It can sometimes feel embarrassing to realize the limitations of my scope or uncomfortable to realize that something I had blown off as no big deal was, in fact, important to someone else. I'm going to sound impossibly old here, but I grew up when the internet was just America Online, and you had to use a landline to plug into the computer. Y'all are navigating so many complex dynamics, and you do it with an ease that is astounding. You ask questions, you educate each other, you are active in politics and social media and creating art. It's incredible.

I believe that learning what you don't know is powerful and beautiful. When you understand what you have left to learn, you can begin to develop those skills. You can become better informed, and your consent can become more finely tuned. And the more you uncover, the more compassionate you can be for others and their journeys, while also maintaining the boundaries you need to feel secure.

Of course, it's not just about the boundaries themselves, or communicating consent before the fact. My hope is that through this journey, you will have learned how to be accountable in ways that help you hurt yourself and those around you less. Like a clown learning how to take a fall, with more practice and introspection, I hope you will be able to take ownership with more grace, which will help those around you to feel safer talking to you. Consent culture is a mutual aid effort, and our individual work can spread to those around us like wildflowers from a seed bomb.

Contrary to what social media or the news wants us to believe, I believe strongly that most people don't come into the world wanting to hurt each other. They become traumatized and scared and lash out, they learn it's effective, and they cycle when traumatized again. "Hurt people hurt people," as the saying goes. Having compassion for people's processes doesn't mean putting up with bullshit, though. I think it's useful to understand, for your own knowledge and for those around you, that not all coping mechanisms are good or healthy, even if they are understandable. You can understand why someone is acting the way they are, and still not want them in your life. That is OK.

Boundaries don't have to be walls, and they don't have to be permanent, but they can become that way if a more flexible fence doesn't suffice. While I believe strongly that most people want to learn and evolve and grow, we must understand that we are not entitled to someone walking alongside us during that process. I think this is important to remember when we're figuring out our own boundaries around a toxic situation, that we are allowed to walk away if we need to or want to. It's also important when we're the ones doing the lashing out and we find ourselves on our own. People who stick with us, telling us the hard truths we don't want to hear while still holding us through the process, are gifts to be valued, not something we are entitled to.

I think most people really do want to do better and be better. They just need a little help figuring out the tools. I hope this book was a helpful tool for you in grappling with the complexity that is consent, and I hope you carry that work forward into your life. Modeling is one of the most effective ways to effect change.

Early in this book, I told a story about reading minds and how frustrating that expectation is, even when I'm the one craving that experience and I know it's fictional. Well, let me give you an example where engaged, attentive communication led to me actually getting what I wanted, no mind reading necessary.

I've been in a situationship for a few months now with a lovely person who asked me early on if they could grab anything for me from the store when I was feeling a little overwhelmed and under the weather. Having had some bad experiences before with having needs in a relationship, I said something like "Oh, no thanks, I don't need anything." This person texted me back, "Sure, you don't *need* anything–but do you *want* anything?" I had to stop and think for a minute–*did* I want anything? I ended up telling them I would actually really like a chocolate cupcake, and thanked them for asking, because having someone go out of their way to do something nice for me makes me feel really cared about.

And you know what? Not only did I get a chocolate cupcake, they actually ask me every once in a while if I want anything, especially when I'm in the middle of writing, or planning an event, or something else big. This isn't because they read my mind–it's because they communicated with me, and I communicated back. Since they feel loved when someone acknowledges the things they do, this date and I have this really wonderful self-perpetuating cycle of kindness and care. I get to be surprised by nice things being done for me, and they get to feel praised and seen.

I wish I had known that was an option when I was a teen. I didn't really have healthy role models for teenage relationships! I just figured that drama and misunderstandings and drawn-out fights were inevitable. Some of it may be, as you figure out how to stand up for yourself, and how to take ownership—being a teenager is a confusing time for most people! But peace and goodwill can also be part of the equation. I hope this book will help you find a little more of those in your own life.

I believe that building a consent culture and thinking critically about what that actually means in practice will help us not only hurt each other less, but also hurt ourselves less. I think people like you are the future. You're having honest conversations my generation couldn't dream of. You are savvy beyond our wildest hopes. It's fucking awesome to watch, and I'm excited to see what you do with this knowledge, and the world.

Keep saying more. Make yourselves heard. Your voices matter.

—Kitty

THERE ARE MANY WAYS TO DEFINE THE FOLLOWING concepts, which you've read about in this book and may hear when talking about consent with other folks. Here is a brief summary of each concept in my own words, from my perspective.

Accountability: Taking ownership of your choices and actions without defensiveness. Often accountability is a combination of acknowledging the situation in words, changing behaviors and making amends in clearly defined ways when appropriate.

Boundary: A clear space or limit between you and another person, where you begin and they end. Boundaries can be physical, emotional, sexual, material or related to time. They can be how close you're willing to get to someone else, and also where you draw the line. A "soft" boundary is one that's a little flexible or fuzzy, while a "hard" boundary is clear-cut.

Calling In: Telling someone in private that something they said or did was harmful. Calling in can be effective when there is trust that your individual disapproval is enough to encourage change, as it feels a little gentler. However, it requires more of your time and labor as you are on your own, and power dynamics can make it uncomfortable if you have less clout than the person you're calling in.

Calling Out: Telling someone in public that something they said or did was harmful. Calling out can be effective when calling in did not work, when you feel you need witnesses to your call for accountability or when you want to demonstrate the community's disapproval. It can lead to defensiveness and aggression on the part of the person being called out, and it can lead to uneven consequences that end up impacting marginalized people more, even when they're not the ones being called out.

Consent: Agreement or permission between people, in which saying "yes" or "no" is equally OK and the participants can give their responses freely, safely and comfortably.

Consent Culture: A social structure focused on increasing opportunities for people to opt in (or opt out) of situations. Consent culture is about moving toward centering consent in interactions, rather than avoiding violation. It's about treating autonomy as sacrosanct and boundaries as valuable information to be respected.

Entitlement Culture: A social structure in which we arrogantly operate under the impression that other people "owe us" unreasonable privileges. I prefer to use this term instead of "rape culture," because I feel it more accurately gets to the root of the problem—people with social advantages feeling they deserve something from others because of that power.

FRIES: Shorthand coined by Planned Parenthood when assessing consent, the FRIES model asks if the consent is:
- Freely given
- Reversible
- Informed
- Enthusiastic
- Specific

Marginalization: When certain groups of people are denied access to basic services or opportunities because they are deemed powerless or unimportant. Marginalization often goes hand in hand with discrimination, particularly for minorities, and can be related to race, ethnicity, economic circumstance, gender, sexual orientation, immigration status, physical or mental ability, weight, age, and many other characteristics. Often, people who are marginalized experience multiple points of marginalization, also known as intersectionality.

Rape Culture: A social structure in which sexual violence (particularly against people who experience misogyny) is normalized, excused away and dismissed—in the media, in the legal system and/or in the culture at large. Often in a rape culture, victims are blamed for their own assaults, and the onus is on avoiding rape instead of on potential rapists not abusing people.

Red Flag: A warning sign that something needs to be dealt with or that a problem needs to be addressed. While this term is often used for assessing others (especially in relationships), in this book I use it to encourage recognizing your own, internal red flags that tell you that something isn't right—feeling queasy in your gut, for example, or wanting to avoid an interaction. A red flag isn't necessarily a dealbreaker in this context, but rather a sign to stop and reflect on how you feel, what's going on and what you need.

Restorative Justice: An ideal about justice that offers the possibility that someone who does harm can learn more, feel empathy and seek to be accountable for that harm. It seeks to center the victim and give them an active role offering input into the process, rather than relying on a corrupt criminal justice system that prefers punishment, retribution and stigma. Restorative justice is an ideal to work toward, in my opinion, rather than a concrete formula.

Social Advantages: Special, unasked-for and unearned positive treatment or value offered only to specific groups by nature of their identity (or perceived identity). It is the counterpart to marginalization. Also called "privilege."

Trigger: A reminder of past trauma that often leads to re-experiencing that trauma in some capacity. Triggers vary wildly and reactions to them can be internally or externally expressed through disassociation, flashbacks and distress. Triggers are often referred to in relation to substance abuse or PTSD, but they can also be related to other mental health issues.

RESOURCES

WHILE I PERSONALLY DO NOT AGREE 100% WITH EVERY-thing presented in all of these resources, I still think they are useful in helping people think critically about the topic at hand. Some are about community activism, some are about romantic relationships and some are about introspective work on your own boundaries. Some are for children, and some are for adults. I wanted to offer resources that would expand your mind, not only around sex and consent, but also about how social issues like race can impact consent, or how to address accountability with your friends. I think there's something to gain from them all, and they've all informed my beliefs. And there's much more out there!

- - - - - - - - - - - - - -

Books and Essays

Be Strong, Be Wise: The Young Adult's Guide to Sexual Assault Awareness and Personal Safety by Amy R. Carpenter

Beyond Survival: Strategies and Stories from the Transformative Justice Movement, edited by Leah Lakshmi Piepzna-Samarasinha and Ejeris Dixon

Can I Give You a Squish? by Emily Neilson

Can We Talk About Consent?: A Book About Freedom, Choices, and Agreement by Justin Hancock and Fuchsia MacAree

Conflict Is Not Abuse: Overstating Harm, Community Responsibility, and the Duty of Repair by Sarah Schulmani

Consent (for Kids!): Boundaries, Respect, and Being in Charge of You by Rachel Brian

Disrupting the Bystander: When #MeToo Happens Among Friends by A.V. Flox

Energetic Boundaries: How to Stay Protected and Connected in Work, Love, and Life by Cyndi Dale

"From White Racist to White Anti-Racist: The Life-Long Journey" by Tema Okun

Learning Good Consent: Building Ethical Relationships in a Complicated World, edited by Cindy Crabb

Let's Talk About It: The Teen's Guide to Sex, Relationships, and Being a Human by Erika Moen and Matthew Nolan

Pleasure Activism: The Politics of Feeling Good by adrienne maree brown

Real Talk about Sex and Consent: What Every Teen Needs to Know by Cheryl M. Bradshaw

So You Want to Talk About Race by Ijeoma Oluo

Speaking from the Heart: 18 Languages for Modern Love by Anne Hodder-Shipp

The Art of Receiving and Giving: The Wheel of Consent by Betty Martin with Robyn Dalzen

The Body Is Not an Apology: The Power of Radical Self-Love by Sonya Renee Taylor

The Five Love Languages: How to Express Heartfelt Commitment to Your Mate by Gary Chapman

Unfuck Your Boundaries: Build Better Relationships through Consent, Communication, and Expressing Your Needs by Faith G. Harper

We Do This 'Til We Free Us: Abolitionist Organizing and Transforming Justice by Mariame Kaba

Yes Means Yes!: Visions of Female Sexual Power and a World without Rape, edited by Jaclyn Friedman and Jessica Valenti

You Too? 25 Voices Share Their #MeToo Stories, edited by Janet Gurtler

- - - - - - -

Websites

Active*Consent: Podcasts, videos and workshops about consent for teens, young adults, parents and caregivers. consenthub.ie

Amaze: Animated videos offering information about healthy social media use, sex and relationships, puberty, and lots more. amaze.org

BISH: A comprehensive collection of articles that can help answer many questions about sex, gender, consent, relationships and more. bishuk.com

Captain Awkward: Excellent advice on communication and boundary setting. captainawkward.com

Comprehensive Consent: Consent skill building for young adults. comprehensiveconsent.com

Go Ask Alice: A website hosted by Columbia University, where a group of educators in different areas answer questions from students. goaskalice.columbia.edu

International Day of Consent (#IDoConsent, November 30): A day to talk about and promote consent culture in and out of the bedroom, started by Jenn Wilson. facebook.com/IDoConsent

Make It About Race: An intersectional approach to teaching about consent by Dr. Nadine Thornhill. nadinethornhill.com/make-it-about-race

Nurturing Human Touch: A starting place for exploring consent and touch. nurturinghumantouch.com

Planned Parenthood for Teens: This national sexual health clinic has a section specifically for teens to get their questions answered. plannedparenthood.org/learn/teens

Queer Sex Ed for All: A subReddit run by Scarleteen. reddit.com/r/QueerSexEdForAll

Scarleteen: A diverse website geared to teenagers that discusses boundaries, sexual health, gender, relationships and more. scarleteen.com

Teen Line: An online and phone resource for teens to talk to other teens about mental health. teenline.org

Teen Vogue: An online magazine for teens and young adults that tackles issues like politics, celebrity culture and more. teenvogue.com

YourTripSister: An Instagram account that shares responsible psychedelic use and education via short videos. instagram.com/yourtripsister

- - - - - - - - - - - - -
Crisis Resources

First Response to Sexual Assault: A flyer with good advice if you find yourself as the first point of contact with a sexual assault survivor. tinyurl.com/305lvan

Kink Aware Professionals: Therapists, doctors and other professionals who have experience with alternative relationships, queerness, polyamory, kink and more, organized by the National Coalition for Sexual Freedom. kapprofessionals.org

National Domestic Violence Hotline: A 24/7 hotline with an extensive resource list organized by state. 1-800-799-SAFE (7233) or TTY 1-800-787-3224, or text "start" to 88788, thehotline.org

Scarleteen: The website also offers a text line, message boards and online chat. 206-866-2279, scarleteen.com/need_help_now_a_guide_to_scarleteens_direct_services

Trans Lifeline: A trans peer support hotline by and for trans folks. U.S: 1-877-565-8860, Canada: 1-877-330-6366, translifeline.org

ASK: BUILDING CONSENT CULTURE

Edited by Kitty Stryker, with a foreword by Laurie Penny

"There are certain conversations that deepen how you think; positively impact how you act; expand your view and understanding of the world, and forever alter how you approach it. This book is full of them. Make room for it–then spread the word."

–Alix Fox, journalist, sex educator and ambassador for the Brook sexual wellbeing charity

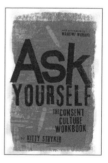

ASK YOURSELF: THE CONSENT CULTURE WORKBOOK

Kitty Stryker, with a foreword by Wagatwe Wanjuki

"*Ask: Building Consent Culture* editor Kitty Stryker invites readers to delve deeper, with guest experts and personal anecdotes, to manifest a culture of consent in one's own community that starts at the heart."

–Jiz Lee, editor of
Coming Out Like a Porn Star

IN IT TOGETHER: NAVIGATING DEPRESSION WITH PARTNERS, FRIENDS, AND FAMILY

JoEllen Notte

"Am I allowed to say I laughed and had so much fun reading about depression? Read this book and you'll feel seen—and you'll walk away with a real-life guide to helping loved ones without sacrificing your own mental health."

—Meredith Goldstein, Boston Globe Love Letters advice columnist, podcast host and author of *Can't Help Myself*

MORE THAN TWO: CULTIVATING NONMONOGAMOUS RELATIONSHIPS WITH KINDNESS AND INTEGRITY

Eve Rickert with Andrea Zanin

Fully revised and updated second edition

A modern topology of nonmonogamy's many possibilities—and consequences.